What's it Worth, Brian?

You Don't Have to be Dead to Have an Estate Sale

By
Brian Lehman
&
Helen Raczuk

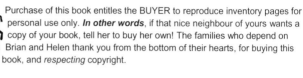

Purchase of this book entitles the BUYER to reproduce inventory pages for personal use only. *In other words*, if that nice neighbour of yours wants a copy of your book, tell her to buy her own! The families who depend on Brian and Helen thank you from the bottom of their hearts, for buying this book, and *respecting* copyright.

For additional copies of this, or other publications,
Email: books@uotter.com
Order on-line: www.uotter.com
Fax   (780) 962-9882
Phone   (780) 962-9854

Cover Photo Credits: Terry Rachuk, Helen Raczuk
Cover Design: Priority Printing

Library and Archives Canada Cataloguing in Publication

Lehman, Brian D., 1946-
    What's it worth, Brian? : you don't have to be dead to have an estate sale / Brian D. Lehman, Helen K. Raczuk.

Includes bibliographical references.
ISBN 0-9731649-4-8

    1. Estate sales. 2. Collectibles. 3. Antiques. I. Raczuk, Helen K., 1952-
II. Title.

HF5482.L44 2004   658.8'7   C2003-905623-6

10 9 8 7 6 5 4 3 2
First Printing, November 2004 Second Printing January 2005
Printed in Canada

Dedication

To little Emma, my mother,
who lived modestly,
had little and always wondered why
Brian needed all 'that' stuff.
She was the best treasure.

Brian

Acknowledgements

We wish to acknowledge Terry Rachuk, without whom, this project would not have happened. We are grateful for his encouragement, support and unwavering faith in us both.

We also wish to acknowledge the lovely Donna, for her perpetual optimism and support.

Gratitude is also extended to the many people who have shared their stories and treasures with us over the past three years, and permitted us to photograph and share them with you.

With deepest gratitude,
Brian & Helen

Brian enjoys the opportunity to help people sort through their stuff and learn more about what they own. He travels extensively to do appraisal events; one of his favorite is the *Brunch with Brian at Bricco* in Calmar  Alberta. Brian is shown here with his friend Terry, the lovely Donna, and Terry's wife Inge (owners of Bricco Ristorante, and co-hosts of the Brunch event).

Table of Contents

How to Use This Book

The intent of this book is to help you take a second look at items you may pass over as worth very little or of no interest, based solely on your own personal taste. *"That's the ugliest lamp I've ever seen!"* only to discover after selling it for $5 at the garage sale that it is really worth $500!

The book is organized to walk you through a home, room by room. Checklists are included to assist you to make an inventory before sorting and making decisions about items. The lists provided are by no means complete and serve as guidelines to help you with that process. Space has been left for you to add your own categories and details, and blank lists are provided for you to copy as needed.

The lists have spaces for you to identify which items to *sell, give away or bequest*. If items are already intended for a particular person, write their name in the

space. Consider taking the completed itemized list and photos to your insurance company, your lawyer and provide a copy for your executor. These detailed lists make their work much easier when it comes to carrying out your wishes or sorting out a claim.

Close-up detail on a biscuit tin dating back to 1930.

Use the pockets to collect and store additional lists, photographs, notes, and other relevant data pertaining to each room. You may also use the pockets to collect advertisements and business cards from experts associated with the sale and inventory.

Some of the more common trademarks, hallmarks, and potters marks, have been included to help you identify your treasures more accurately. Entire volumes are devoted to hallmarks alone, so once you know how to look, consult library books to get more information about dating and identifying pieces.

Pictures are included of treasures Brian has seen at some of his estate and appraisal events and are typical of items which may be in your home. Because the market is always shifting, values have not been given for every item, however, values noted are for insurance replacement only and are not to be considered selling prices. The market for many collectibles and antiques often depends on the age of the buyers and what is currently popular in the decorating and collecting world. On the other hand, some things will always be valuable. It is best to consult an accredited appraiser for advice about values for both insurance and resale.

> *5 years ago, Betty found two blue horse figurines dumped into a grab box at a garage sale. One was in fine condition, the other missing a leg but it was also in the box. Betty took the pair, and had the leg repaired. The Beswick equine duo, even with repairs, is valued at $3600 .*

Introduction
Philosophy

It's great fun to turn a plate over, look at the markings and hear the appraiser say, "*This is unbelievable! I never thought I would see one of these in my lifetime.*" Your heart pounds in your ears as you strain to hear the next part. You know the number he is about to announce will be more than you possibly could have imagined. All kinds of thoughts run through your mind as you rethink your plan to take Grandmother's plate out to the cottage. This old plate may become the most beautiful thing you own because someone else has recognized what it's really worth.

Rosenthal tray, Handpainted, from 1896 - 1906. If you find one like this, set it aside for a professional appraisal. Definitely worth it.

"*Are you going to use this plate?*" Brian asks.

"*Oh no. It might be too valuable, and I'd be afraid something would happen to it.*"

"*Well, then,*" Brian continues, "*I'm not going to tell you what it's worth.*"

You're stunned! How could he do this to you? Simple. Brian Lehman believes that beautiful things are meant to be used and enjoyed. Because they are used, they are valued. True, everyone seems to have the good dishes and the everyday dishes, but to actually use the good set without always having a good reason is what Brian encourages everyone to do. You acquired the pieces because you love them so what are you waiting for? Use them! You're worth it.

"OK - I promise, I will use the plate."
"Good. Then let me tell you about this plate."

You listen, and realize that the plate has a story. You learn about the artist, the company and the period of time in which the plate was produced. You might even learn that it's not intended to be used as a plate but for something else! You think to yourself - *"Grandma loved it because it was pretty. It didn't occur to her that it would be valuable someday. She wanted me to have it because she loved it, and hoped I would love it too. I will use it, think of her, and honour her memory."*

Will you use Grandma's plate? Of course you will. In doing so, you will cherish the memories, and cherish the giver. It is now a part of your history and you can pass it on to someone else who values the memory as much as the plate.

▲ Top: Bavarian plate, turn of the century, handles, gold trim.

◄ Left: Thomas, Bavaria, circa 1908 Value: $75 - $125

Both are fine examples of hand painted porcelain plates.

What is an Estate sale ?

Contrary to popular belief, you don't have to be dead to have an estate sale. Unlike a garage sale where the intent is to find more room in the closets and cupboards, the purpose of an estate sale is to sell items of quality, which in most cases include two to three generations of inherited items taking up valuable space. That means selling vintage linens, estate jewelry, good quality furniture, treasured collectibles and artwork; items you may have inherited or collected through the years but no longer use.

Reasons to have an estate sale:

Dispose of an estate of someone who has died.

When someone dies, an estate sale is one of the ways to disperse and dispose of that estate. In addition to the contents of a home which reflect the accumulation of an entire life, the property might also be sold. The intent of this type of estate sale is to sell everything, right down to the teaspoons and doorknobs. Generally, arrangements are made between the executor and the family members. Family members deal first with bequeathed items. Once all those details are sorted, and all bequests satisfied, then plans can begin for an estate sale. Considerable care and planning needs to take place before the sale can occur.

As an executor, you have been entrusted with the task of disposing of the house and the contents. This is an enormous responsibility. Having the authority to act on behalf of the deceased means you need to *do what is right.*

You are entrusted to honour the wishes of the deceased, and protect their desires with the respect and dignity that is rightfully theirs.

An estate sale can be emotionally exhausting and highly stressful because of all the details. You will need to contact family members for bequeathed items and to give them first choice of other items. Possessions need to be sorted and many decisions made. Don't attempt to do this alone. At some point you will need to call on an expert to assist you. A third party serves as a buffer between you and well meaning neighbours, friends and relatives seeking special deals.

Don't Rush! *Take the time to mourn.* Take time to meet your memories and be respectful of the life that has just passed. Use time to your advantage.

One of the biggest mistakes people make early on when settling an estate is to rush into decisions which are often driven by emotion and pressure to *get on with your life*. Many people are in a hurry to sell everything, including the house. It has been around for forty or fifty years already; another month won't alter its marketability. Rather than consult a real estate agent right away, or contract a store owner or dealer to clear the house, (not recommended), follow this simple format:

> ***Brian Says:***
>
> It is not a good idea to contact a store owner or dealer for appraisals as they are buyers and do not always have your best interests at heart. When looking for an appraiser, find one not connected with any kind of shop.

1. Clean out the fridge and check for other potentially perishable items and discard.
2. Do not disconnect the phone. You need it .
3. Leave the cable connected because that will help to sell the television.

4.   Change the locks to eliminate the possibility of theft by unscrupulous relatives.

5.   Make sure the insurance is up to date and check that there is enough content insurance.

6.   Buy two *BEWARE OF THE DOG* signs. Put one in the front window, and another at the back door. It makes thieves think twice.

7.   Don't wash anything. Don't repair anything (unless it impacts security). Once things have settled down, then decisions can be made. (see **Walking Through the House,** page 21)

8.   You can hire home inspectors to check up on the house once a day for four - six weeks for nominal fees. Do NOT give a key to the neighbours.

9.   Take time to grieve. Allow yourself time to get through the rough parts. Things will get done. Remember, tears are the highest form of respect you can pay.

Dispose of an estate to enable a move to a seniors residence or medical facility

Circumstances have arisen that necessitate moving your parent into a seniors residence or care facility. How do you condense more than seventy years of living to fit into a tiny assisted living space, or three room suite? The task is overwhelming.

Time for an estate sale. This is a sale that cannot be arranged overnight. If you can see this coming, give yourself lots of time to plan. You have been entrusted to do what is right and what is best for your parent. Careful consideration of other family members is necessary before you start tagging and selling. Expert assistance is definitely required to make this process as painless and as lucrative as possible. The contents of the home belong to your parents. It is nice to be able to provide them with the financial rewards of fifty-plus years of living.

A move like this can take up to two years to materialize. Waiting lists are the primary reason for huge delays in making a move. Put your name on the lists and take advantage of time to plan. Set aside what your parents wish to take with them. Use green dots to identity items as *Keepers*, then decide what to do with the rest. Sort into zones: *Donate*, *Kids*, or *Sell*. Keep in mind that in the lifetime of the home, the value of the contents has also increased.

Downsizing

The kids have grown up, gone their own way and are finally out of the house! Time to get that two bedroom condo and spend the winters in warmer climes, or better yet, move into the RV and hit the open road.

However, before that can happen, furniture needs to be sold. There are sets of dishes that the kids don't want and a lifetime accumulation of unused birthday gifts, inheritances, and boxes of stuff you've collected that would be better off elsewhere! An estate sale is definitely appropriate!

This is the best kind of an estate sale because it is not tied to anyone else's emotion but your own and is not pressured by time constraints. If at all possible, start planning and preparing at least one or two years in advance. Live through all the seasons carefully considering and planning what stays, what goes, what gives! Try to establish one room to collect all the unwanted items, adding to the collection as you continue to sort and identify them.

The best way to prepare for this sale is to start clearing things away. (see the **Toss-It List** on page 23) Get a dozen or so new lidded boxes and label them: *Keep, Give to Charity, Give to Family* (label name) *Sell, Recycle, Trash.* Put items into the appropriate box. Go through the boxes occasionally, and remind yourself that even though it is hard to let go of some stuff, there are no china cabinets in heaven! General rule is: *if you can't recall the last time you used an item, chances are you don't need it.* It can go. Stack the boxes until you are ready to start moving things out.

Redecorating or Renovating

The last of the kids has moved out and it is finally safe to convert that bedroom into the library you've

---

Sorting Boxes
Keep
Give to Charity
Give to Family (label name)
Sell
Recycle
Trash

---

always wanted. You're knocking out a wall to expand the dining room because you expect to have dinners for children and grandchildren, right? But before you start, there's a little matter of the furniture, old toys and other things that really should go.

There's nothing wrong with the old bedroom suite, or the kitchen dishes, but a garage sale just won't work. Garage sale shoppers expect to find deals for fifty cents. Those old cups and saucers are worth much more than that, as is your lamp and Grandma's easy chairs. An estate sale is the perfect way to get what they're worth. It's a great opportunity to get extra funds to decorate your newly renovated home.

Changes in family status or life style
Divorce
Inheritance
Marriage
Relocating for a new job

In these situations, you have either accumulated someone else's things, or are in the process of disposing of your own. Either way, possessions need to be sorted, appraised, and sold before you can move on. A moving sale is best, but expert assistance is still needed to appraise, organize and set up the sale. It is really important to have items appraised BEFORE you start selling. All too often, people price an item for quick sale only to be shocked later when they learn the item was far more valuable than they could have imagined. Seek expert advice. It's worth it.

Consider combining a house sale with the estate sale because both sales attract prospective buyers for the other event. A partially furnished home is much more attractive to potential home buyers than one that is completely bare.

Pare down to what you want to take. If possible, move the possessions you wish to keep into your new home, and leave the rest for the sale. When you have the sale, it shows the home to its best advantage. If you have all the rest cleared and organized, you are better prepared for the house-buyer who wishes to take immediate possession.

Brian Says:
Use the house to sell the contents and the contents to sell the house.

Did you know that the term *flea market* likely originated from the fact that old, used stuff was probably infested with the little beasties. Fortunately, most flea markets no longer have that problem, but you should still take care with old clothing, paper and other bio-degradable products. Check carefully before making a purchase.

Why Get an Appraiser?

An appraiser will give you fair market values on items destined for sale. These values are documents which can be used for insurance purposes as well as for estate valuations. The appraiser recognizes value, and is knowledgeable about the current trends in the market. He knows what collectors want and what they are prepared to pay. He may also be able to recommend reliable and qualified people for repairs and restoration. It is inconceivable that you will sell absolutely everything, so he can also advise where unsold items can go. You have already decided to part with these things and you don't want to incorporate them back into your life, so prepare to be rid of them at the end of the sale.

The services of an appraiser are really valuable in the long run. He will save you time, money and anxiety during a process which is typically full of anxiety, and short on money and time. Be wary of the person who offers to help you appraise items for free, or in exchange for goods. Also be cautious of someone associated with a shop who offers to buy or resell your possessions for you. An appraiser should NOT offer to purchase any items you wish to sell. One who does so definitely does not have your best interests as their primary concern. This is a conflict of interest and is highly unethical.

The phone lists all kinds of appraisers but you may wish to contact one who is a member of the CPPA group (Certified Personal Property Appraiser) in your area.

Before The Appraiser Comes ...

Is Your House Sick?

No matter how much you want to believe your parents were immaculate housekeepers, the fact is that unless they had access to professional assistance, things are no longer up to their usual demanding standards. Chances are corners have been missed because of aching hands, failing eyesight and lack of energy. Don't despair, but do prepare! Working in dust is really bad for your own health. As you work hard, you perspire, wipe your face and eyes and spread spores. Eventually, this may result in serious eye infections and sinus problems that soon escalate into respiratory problems. Take proper steps to

---

Brian says:

Annette and Ed had lived in their home for 36 years. It was small but cozy, with hardwood floors, wooden cupboards, wooden shutters. After a sale, they moved into a seniors residence. All was well for about two months when both started having breathing problems. The culprit? The formaldehyde in the new wall to wall broadloom., the off gases from the cupboards and not being accustomed to air conditioning.

---

protect yourself. You are not insulting your parents. You are being realistic and using common sense. Before commencing your walk through the house:

1. Change the furnace filter immediately, then every month thereafter until the work is complete.
2. Check the humidifier and either replace or remove the unit. Both furnace and humidifier are perfect breeding grounds for germs, spores and mites. Once you start moving things around, you will also be stirring up the germs, spores and mould, pet hairs and other unhealthy critters. You may end up with serious allergy, breathing or skin reactions. To protect yourself, you should:

    a. Purchase a mask, goggles (they can fit over glasses), heavy duty rubber gloves OR

    b. Hire a professional cleaning crew if the task is overwhelming or impractical for you to manage.

In the same way that clearing out an older established residence can be hazardous to your health, the same can be said for moving into a new residence. Brand new carpeting, paint, numerous glues and varnishes throw off-gases which can affect breathing.

The greatest problem for most seniors is respiratory. In some cases, the healthier alternative may be to keep parents in their own home. They've become accustomed to the environment in which they have been living, and moving may upset that balance. Give the house a thorough professional cleaning at least once a year and arrange for homecare to tend to basic daily needs. Doing this will reduce countless doctor visits to determine why Mom and Dad are listless, wheezing, and generally in ill health since the *big move*.

Brian says:

Brian met a couple who had just purchased a stately Victorian home. Shortly after they moved in, their dogs began to react strangely. They scratched, and were not behaving in a healthy fashion. A visit to the vet revealed the pets had fleas! The couple was puzzled, but upon further examination of their new home, discovered the carpets were infested with fleas. Disinfecting the carpets was not a solution. All carpets had to be completely removed, rooms disinfected, and new flooring installed. The previous owner, who had three dogs and two cats, drove past shortly after the renovation and noticing that the carpets had been removed, asked if he could take them for his home!

Moral of the story? Before moving your parents (or yourself) into another home, first check on the health of the home. Take the time to clean thoroughly, disinfect and if necessary, repaint and replace carpeting, re-do tiling and grout or completely replace bathroom fixtures.

Called a sad iron or a flat iron, the handle on this model detaches enabling one to exchange the cooled iron for one heating on the stove. Usually these have ended up as doorstops or bookends.

Walking Through the House

The first walk through gives an overview of the whole situation. Make a list of the big stuff (furniture, appliances, things on the wall.) Photograph each and every room from all angles. Include several items in one shot. Include furniture measurements on the back of the photos. If you are moving, take the photos with you when home-shopping, to remind yourself what kind of furniture needs to fit into the rooms. The photos also serve as an instant inventory check after you move, should something go astray in the move.

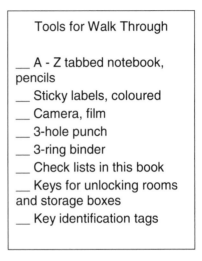

Tools for Walk Through

___ A - Z tabbed notebook, pencils
___ Sticky labels, coloured
___ Camera, film
___ 3-hole punch
___ 3-ring binder
___ Check lists in this book
___ Keys for unlocking rooms and storage boxes
___ Key identification tags

Sort through cupboards and drawers as suggested for each of the rooms and make more detailed lists. Now you should have a good idea of the whole situation and are ready to contact an appraiser to set up a meeting. You have done a great deal of work so that you can ask questions, and give informed answers from your lists! Most appraisers can quickly determine, if you qualify for an estate sale.

The Valuables

When you begin your initial inventory of china, look for backstamps. Check the marks on pages 57 - 59 to see if you have any that match. If you know you have an entire cabinet of Royal Doulton or a box of old Dresden plates, bring those out for the appraiser. Do some sorting, but don't pile it all on the dining room table! Make lists of quantity and function of pieces in sets.

The more homework done at this stage, the better in the long run, for once the appraiser comes in, he's on the clock and will be much more efficient if some of the preliminary sorting has been already done. If you do hire professional help to organize your sale, a toss-and-sort-day should be included. Remember not to throw out dishes or ceramics without any markings on the back. No markings often means the items are older than 1891!

Documentation

As you go through drawers and files, and piles of paper, you may come across old manuals, warranties, and sales slips. Don't toss them out just yet. They may match up with something packed away in the attic or stuck in the back of a cupboard. An original instruction book, sales slip or box can dramatically add value to an item. Even a dated catalogue advertising an item and the original list price adds to the value. Compile everything in a three-ring binder for future reference.

Each room has its own unique challenges; from furniture and ornaments to contents of drawers and cupboards. Organize the walk logically to alleviate frustration and a feeling of helplessness! Do all the big stuff first, then move to what's on display, then into drawers and shelves and so on. Keep notes of where you've been, and the job won't be nearly so exhausting.

Throw it Away!

CAUTION - Tossing may become habit forming. Don't attempt to do this all in one day or even in one week. If you have the luxury of time on your side, use it to your advantage otherwise indiscriminate tossing occurs and costly mistakes may result. HOWEVER, there are some things that must be tossed. Most of our parents and grandparents were raised during a time when saving was considered frugal and clever. Times have changed. A lot of things can be recycled and some things just really ought to go!

Toss-it list

Food containers
Old sticky plastic containers are not nice, especially plastic bags leftover from grocery stores, old Tupperware and washed out zipper bags.

Tin Cans
Tin containers, like coffee cans and tobacco tins aren't valuable. Rusty tins definitely have no value unless they are more than 60 years old.

Sealers
Canning jars can be donated or recycled unless they have turned a bluish-turquoise colour or a violet colour. Wait and have those checked. They may be worth something. Also watch for jars with BEAVER images on them.

Wire hangers
Some dry cleaners might recycle these.

Fabric remnants
Donate remnants only if they are big enough to actually be useful. Quilting groups might appreciate a bag of clean fabric remnants.

Magazines
Occasionally, you will find ads of people offering to purchase old magazines. These need to be in excellent condition to be of value. If they aren't, then recycle. However, do keep LIFE, LOOK and SATURDAY EVENING POST. Values are often determined by who is on the cover and the great advertising inside.

Building Supplies
Bits of boards, nails, screws, and jars of nuts and bolts can be sent to the scrap heap or fire pit.

Gardening Supplies
Garden hoses, gardening pots and trays, opened bags of fertilizer, pesticides, soils and so forth can be disposed. Fertilizers lose their value after they have been opened for a time and can pose a serious health hazard. Dispose of these safely.

Stoneware crocks, such as this Dyson's Pickles crock, are a common find in many prairie farm homes. Nearly every homemaker made pickles and sauerkraut from their garden harvest in preparation for winter meals ahead. Because these are so common, their value is mostly aesthetic or sentimental, rather than monetary.
Value: $50-75

Seed Packets

Unless you encounter unopened seed packets that are vintage (more than thirty years) they have no value. Old seed packets are actually collectible items, but only for the art on the package, and even then the value is minimal. The seeds only have a shelf life of two years.

All perishable and open food packages

Plumbing materials

Everyone has a used tap or old toilet seat tucked in a corner somewhere. Definitely not a keeper. Toss it!

Old windows and window screens

Unless they are still useful for the house, they can be discarded. No one will use these. An exception is stained or leaded glass, regardless of the condition.

Toxic Materials

Paint cans, cleaners, aerosol cans, batteries; all these must be disposed of safely. Check with the local fire department for the location of a toxic-waste disposal station.

Cardboard Boxes

Original boxes for some items are fine to keep especially for games, toys, and antique Christmas ornaments. However corrugated boxes, especially from food, should be sent to the recycle centre. Purchase new boxes for packing to ensure spores, germs and other nasties that have taken up residence in old, musty cardboard are not coming to the new house with you.

Papers

For legal purposes, and for the preservation of family history, several documents MUST be kept. Marriage certificates, baptismal certificates, death certificates, citizenship papers, awards and academic diplomas, are just a few of the documents that must be safely stored. Sort through those and get assistance from an archival expert regarding methods of safely and properly preserving them. Get a safety deposit box for the really important documents. Allocate a binder or portable security file for the rest of the important family documents. If other papers have valuable information, consider reproducing it digitally or preserving it in a frame or in a format recommended by archival experts. Other family members might be interested in having copies. Some papers may be of value to a local museum, especially if they contribute significantly to local history.

Dancing figurine by Freda Doughty. Listen carefully and you can almost hear the music. This charming couple is designed and painted in exquisite detail. From the flowers in the little girl's hair, to the buckles on the little boy's shoes and the grass beneath their feet, the art work is impressive and deserves to be displayed and admired.

Brian Says:

This entire section has been devoted to the preparation of the residence for departure. Perhaps it is not really necessary for a move. Whose convenience is being addressed? Consider comfort, security, and health and safety of the senior. Perhaps their care can best be attended to by bringing in people to assist with homecare, food preparation, recreation, and companionship and entertainment.

Often, decisions to move out are made hastily, especially after the death of one parent. Unless there are serious health concerns and safety risks that necessitate a move, keeping Mom and Dad in their home may better serve the quality of their life in the long run.

◀Ringer attachment for washtubs made washday much easier for the modern homemaker of the early 1900's. Approximate value: $50 Often used for display purposes only.

Additional Items	Keep	Sell	Bequest

The Living Room

The living room was not always a room for living. Before funeral homes took on the task of taking care of the deceased, each family would care for their own. The Parlor, as it was often called, was used almost exclusively for viewing the deceased and for important family gatherings. Once funeral homes became the norm, the Parlor took on a new life, and become a room for the living.

▲A Victorian mahogany carved open armchair with button back, supported on china castors.
Value: $1500

◄A prayer chair (Prie Dieux) is not commonly found in modern homes. This one originally belonged in a country church, and was saved from a fire. One kneels on the seat of the chair, which is low to the floor, and holds a prayer book, or folds hands on the back to pray. This one has the original rush seat. Some are more ornate with tapestry or velvet cushions. Value: $750—$1000 if a true antique.

living room	Keep	Sell	Bequest
Furniture			
Books			
Rugs			
Lamps			
Fixtures			

living room	Keep	Sell	Bequest
Photos			
Paintings			
Tapestries			
Prints			
Figurines			
Musical			
Instruments			
Other			

Furniture

Design and Style

Style is influenced by the general interest and market appeal of a particular era. Rococo, William and Mary, Edwardian, Victorian, Art Deco, Shaker, and Country are just some of the many styles that reflect a period of our history. While modern furniture makers attempt to copy the old masters, newer furniture is mass produced and lacks some of the unique techniques earlier masters used in the construction of the piece.

Attempting to restore a piece by re-upholstering, re-finishing or repairing, (glue guns are NOT a good idea!) will seriously affect the value, and the quality of the piece. Some furniture simply needs a good cleaning. Consult an expert to get an estimate for repair and restoration, then decide whether or not the cost is justified.

Hardwood frame, brocade upholstery, typical arm chair from the 1930's.
Value: $500 or more

If the pile on your rugs has been dented by furniture legs, leave an ice-cube to melt in the hollow, then vacuum dry. Also check the backs of cupboards and drawers, tile grouting and shower curtains for mould and mildew. Loosen these black stains by holding a boiling kettle or a steaming iron against them, then wipe clean.

cleaning tip

◄A tea trolley, such as this one, made casual entertaining much easier. The table was wheeled out as needed, set, and tea was served. Cherry wood was a favorite wood because of its rich red colour. This drop-leaf table is from 1930, and the design makes storage convenient for smaller living rooms.
Value: $500 or more

►Gateleg table, hardwood stained walnut colour. Could be expanded to a full size table. 1930

▼1930 Davenport, hardwood frame with rosy pink brocaded upholstery.

Light Fixtures
Repairing and Rewiring

There are at least three things wrong with the rewiring that has been done to this Galle lamp, which is one sign that it is a modern reproduction.

Light fixtures must be carefully rewired for function and safety. This particular lamp, with an insurance value of $450, was incorrectly rewired and the incorrect bulb size installed. When rewiring old lamps, use reproduced vintage cords and plugs.

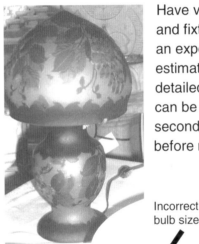

Have vintage and antique lamps and fixtures properly restored by an expert. Always request an estimate which should include a detailed outline of precisely what can be done and the cost. Get a second or even third opinion before making a final decision.

Incorrect
bulb size

Exposed wires

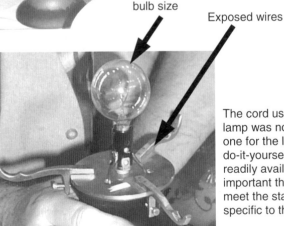

The cord used on this lamp was not the correct one for the lamp. While do-it-yourself kits are readily available, it is important that wiring meet the standards specific to the lamp.

To Clean or Not to Clean:
An Enlightening Story

A lady was at an appraisal event, holding a copper lamp which she had polished and cleaned especially for the appraisal. The lamp caught the attention of an appraiser who identified it as a hand hammered copper lamp from the studio of Dick Van Erp a well known San Francisco artist. Value? $50 - $60,000. Had she NOT cleaned it, the value would have been in excess of $150,000.

◄Lamps like this banquet lamp, or

►milky white glass with rosy red and pink painted roses don't come up very often, but when they do, they are worth a second look. Bases are often mismatched with bulbs or shades making them difficult to appraise and authenticate.

Brass and Copper

Vintage brass or copper fixtures are highly sought after items by collectors and designers. To meet the market demand, reproductions are being mass-produced and are often sold for exorbitant prices to the unsuspecting buyer. Old is in. Beware when you buy that you are getting the real antique, or if it is a reproduction that it is clearly marked as such. Be suspicious of brass or copper that is shiny. Usually it has a lacquer finish which old brass and copper does not. Most brass reproductions are worth very little. Many items marked *INDIA* are also modern; early 20th century and mass produced. Any items stamped *CHINA*, however, are worth a second look.

> ### Brian Says
> *Did you know that rubbing a piece of brass with Pledge will give it a shine, prevent additional tarnish and not destroy the patina!*

While it is tempting to clean up a piece, the charm and warmth of a piece of vintage metal is in the patina, or the aged and worn finish.

Figurines

Before you dismiss all those fussy ornaments and vases as worthless dust collectors, take a second look. There should be a trademark on the bottom. Some of the more common and interesting ones have been included throughout this book, to help you identify some pieces that may worth keeping. However, this list is by no means complete!

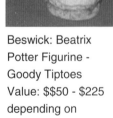

Beswick: Beatrix Potter Figurine - Goody Tiptoes Value: $$50 - $225 depending on backstamp.

You may be surprised what you might discover! Figurines that are highly collectible are often from a limited edition series. Figurines from popular literature, such as Beatrix Potter's *Peter Rabbit* stories, classics like *Winnie The Pooh*, and Disney characters are also quite collectible. Even more desirable are complete collections. For example, the complete series of Snow White figurines will bring more than one or even a few of the pieces. If display pieces are part of the set, the entire collection may be very valuable. Look for markings of *Wade, Royal Doulton, Beswick, Hummel, Goebel, Coalport, Royal Worchester, Iladro, Bunnykins, Dresden,* and *Armani* as some of the pieces worth keeping or purchasing.

◄Etched detail on a green glass vase. A stunning piece that is tempting to display in a bright sunny spot to appreciate the colour and beauty of the glass. Be careful with this temptation, however, as damage to furniture could happen as strong sun passes through glass leaving burn marks on the surface of the wood. Mary Gregory type vase, value up to $350, depending on size and authenticity.

►Royal Doulton has made a number of figurines celebrating famous people and recognizing a number of fashions from different eras. They have also created different series to celebrate literary figures, historic figures and popular celebrities.
Most are made in limited editions, and once retired may fetch very high prices, depending on original demand of the piece and the quantity made. Get advice to value these pieces.

cleaning tip

Cleaning Tip

Although aged pieces are desirable, dust and dirt detract from the beauty of a figurine. Often, detailed figurines are not purchased or are quickly discarded because of their dirty appearance. Fear not! There is a solution to cleaning and restoring them to their original luster.

DO NOT use chemical cleaners on porcelain, glass, or china. Use a fine paint brush, or an airbrush to clear out collected dust. If necessary, you can also use a soft toothbrush to dislodge some of the dust, but don't scrub!

Wash porcelain and pottery in the same manner as you would fine china. Use a liquid hand soap with none or little PH. Avoid dishwashers at all costs, because the detergent and high pressure of the water will damage any gold design, and scratch and scuff the glaze.

If something is badly stained, line a sink with a towel or use a plastic bin. Fill it with lukewarm water to completely cover the item and add a mild detergent. (do NOT use bleach!) Lay the items down carefully, one at a time. Soak. Turn the item upside down, swish it from side to side then rinse and allow to drip dry.

A collection of Hummel figurines is attractively displayed. The common theme linking these charming figures makes this a peaceful and happy setting.

The Story of Hummel

The F. W. Goebel factory was founded in 1871 by Franz and William Goebel in Oeslau, Germany. In 1935, the signature of M.I Hummel first appeared on a figurine. The company began making limited edition plates in 1971. These were made, numbered, and then the molds destroyed. Figurines, however, were not always made in limited editions and are occasionally reintroduced. Collectors are more concerned about marks on Hummels than on most figurines. The mark is the way the age of a piece is established. This age, and the size of the piece determines the value. To a collector, the earliest examples are more valuable than current ones. Markings with any variation of the bee, are the best. Generally, the bigger the bee, the older the piece.

▲ Goebel Crown
1935 - 1949

▲ 1950-59
Full Bee

1960 - 1963

Berta Hummel met William Goebel when she was sixteen enroute to Berlin. He saw great promise in sketches she'd made of childhood friends and had them transformed into figurines. Berta entered a convent and became Maria Inocensia Hummel. After that, the marking most often found on her designs is *M.I. Hummel* which is highly collectible. Her untimely death from pneumonia at the age of 35 only ensured enduring popularity of her work. In tribute to her, figurines after her death are called Goebels and prior to her death are known as Hummels.

▲ Goebel
Hummel three
line mark
1964 - 1972

▲ Goebel
Trademark
2000 - present

Pottery or Porcelain?

Pottery is

* thicker than porcelain
* made in a variety of colors
* usually found in kitchens for utilitarian function
* doesn't 'ring' when thwacked on the rim with a finger
* porous - so is glazed inside, to hold liquid

Porcelain is

* hard and glassy, not porous
* white in colour
* translucent (hold it up to the light, the light will sometimes shine through)
* resonant - especially if it is a bowl shape
* decoration will be hand painted or applied by transfer

Pottery and Porcelain

Crazing

Very fine cracks in the glaze. This is expected in pieces that are very old or have suffered from years of neglect. It cannot be corrected. Take fine china if it is not used often, and soak it in warm water periodically.

▲ Delftware vase from 1930

Limited Edition

Highly collectible. After a piece is made, the mold is destroyed. Must have total quantities made identified, not total 'firing' days.

Delft

It is a misconception that all Delft is Dutch. It is actually made in several countries, England and Germany but mostly Holland, Designs of flowers, ships, and windmills are usually in blue on white background. This is not to be confused with Blue Willow which is also mostly blue on white. The English version of blue and white pottery is called delftware.

Art Nouveau

This style of art was developed in the late nineteenth century. Designs are curvilinear and based on natural forms.

Iridescent

A glaze on glass and porcelain that has a colourful sheen to it. Think of oil on water to get a sense of what this looks like. Tiffany is best known for use of this glaze.

▲ Art Deco basket from 1930

Bisque

is porcelain that has only been fired once and not glazed. It has a soft grainy look making it appealing for doll faces and hands. When used for figurines it is often painted. Bisque doll faces with closed mouths are the most valuable!

Art Deco

is a design style that is associated with the 1920's. It is sleek, with minimal lines and smooth shapes. This style is found in everything from lamps and glassware, to dishes and jewelry.

Hard Paste, Soft Paste

Hard paste is much stronger and smoother, and if chipped, the unglazed surface appears smooth, unlike soft paste which is more grainy in appearance. Hard paste porcelain is desirable because of its resistance to stains and heat. When tapped on the edge, really fine porcelain will have a clear ring to it. If there is a dull thud, then the piece has been damaged and may have a hairline crack somewhere.

▲ Danish Art Nouveau vase by Bing & Groendahl from early 1900

◀This particular Moorcroft vase from about 1920, with bright red and yellow leaf designs on a black background may look ordinary to the untrained eye, but is amongst items on the collector's hot list. The marking on the bottom is quite prominent but size of vessel, type of flower, and colour of the written signature determines the age and value.
Value: $300

Nippon is the name Japan used on porcelain and china 1891-1921. After that time, 'Made in Japan' appeared. Noritake is a Japanese ware made in 1904 by Nippon Toki Kaisha. It is still being made today.

Displaying Figurines

Why hide the figurine in a china cabinet or worse yet; leave it wrapped up in a box under the bed! Display it on a table, so that all views can be admired and appreciated. Purchase a bell glass cover, available in fine china and antique shops, to protect it from dust but make it easily accessible to admiring eyes.

Reproductions: Buyer Beware

Many old marks are being reproduced on new pieces. Although not foolproof, as rule of thumb, if the backstamp appears outside the glazing (on the surface), BEWARE. If you can *feel* the mark with your fingernail, it is definitely a reproduction. If it appears hazy and beneath the layers of glaze, it may be a genuine product. Be especially vigilant with pieces labeled: *Limoges, Bavarian, Nippon, Noritake, RS Prussia /Germany, Roseville*.

These two reclining felines are almost identical in appearance, however one is a Beswick (bottom, value: $50) and the other is a very close reproduction made in Japan (top, value: $20) Fortunately, both are clearly marked.

►Wade Heath pitcher, woodland bunny and bird design in greens and browns. This treasure was found in a cabin. New owners had it appraised and were surprised to find this 1936 -1948 piece valued at $225 or more.

Furniture

Veneer was the finish of choice for most furniture made during the 20's and 30's. Since solid hardwoods were extremely expensive, veneers were dyed to resemble expensive woods. Most often, mahogany or cherry wood was used. Occasionally, old veneer will chip or blister, and expert assistance is needed to repair the damage. Some older pieces have been stained or painted numerous times, and removing those finishes also requires expert assistance, otherwise it could result in the veneer lifting completely off the base.

▶ Three-tiered mahogany table, typical of the 1930's and found in many parlors or living rooms. Also popular were nesting tables, plant tables, tables with magazine troughs, and chair or end tables. A table like this provided ample space to display knick-knacks, a beautiful plant, a lamp, and perhaps a few family photographs.

▼ Burl walnut veneer end table, 1930. Value: $125 - $175, depending on condition.

▶ Leather tooled top on a mahogany veneer base. This occasional table from 1930 was perfect when additional space was required for visitors to set their tea cups. Some of these tables had a tilt-top which made storage convenient when not in use.

The Dining Room

1920 walnut veneer buffet with burl walnut veneer doors. Part of a full eight piece dining set. Depending on condition, value can be as high as $1500.

At one time, everyone ate from a common bowl; men ate first, then the women and finally the children. Utensils were not yet developed, so fingers were the tool of choice for scooping food out of the bowl. Eventually, a wooden or bone spoon was invented.

In Mediaeval times, men carried a knife with them, which was used for protection, hunting, and as the main eating utensil. By the 1300's, the fork came into use. People began to eat from individual plates, had their own cup, used napkins (not sleeves!) and it was no longer acceptable to toss the bones onto the floor! Tools and utensils were perfected and invented as the need arose, resulting in some interesting and unusual culinary utensils which collectors seek today.

Dining Room	Keep	Sell	Bequest
Furniture			
Rugs			
China and Porcelain			

Dining Room	Keep	Sell	Bequest
Pictures			
Paintings			
Tapestries			
Other			
Collectibles			
Figurines			
Silver			
Brass			
Pewter			
Copper			
Heirloom			
Tablecloths			
Needlework			
Other			

Sterling and Silver

Victorians had a great deal of time on their hands, it seems, because they created a piece of cutlery for every conceivable dish to serve and eat. Some settings can have up to fourteen pieces of cutlery for each person! For example: cream soup spoon, or clear broth soup spoon, coffee spoon, tea spoon, dessert spoon. Confusing to use, confusing to set but stunning to see all laid out for a sumptuous feast. In some cultures a proper setting consists of no less than twenty-two pieces.

As the awareness of cleanliness and health increased, so too did the concern for the kind of manners and behaviours that were acceptable around the dining table. The Victorians carried table manners and use of utensils to extremes. Numerous books have been written detailing the proper procedure for everything from who should sit where to what utensils should be used to eat different foods. (fish fork, salad fork)

This silver marrow scoop from 1745, or these salt shovels from 1775 are some of the unique utensils no longer found on the modern table.

Hallmarks

Although English silver has been hallmarked since the Middle Ages, the practice of including a town mark, maker's mark and a date letter became standard practice around 1260. Hallmarking developed around 1470 to maintain a standard of fineness of gold and silver and to curb frauds committed by the goldsmiths. Goldsmiths had to take their silver and gold items to the Goldsmiths' Hall to be tested and marked, thus the origin of *Hallmark*. Date cycles were changed annually, with the letters representing a 20 year cycle (letter J is omitted, and the cycle ends at U). The format of the letter also changed when the cycle changed.

◀Sterling Silver Hallmark

▶Gold Hallmark

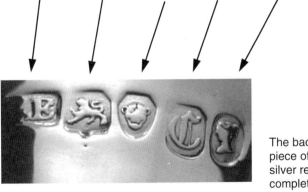

The back of a piece of sterling silver reveals a complete history of that piece. The marks indicate maker, purity of silver or gold, place of origin, and date. The duty mark, originally created to show that a tax had been paid to the crown, ceased to be used after 1890.

Sterling

is solid silver. You know it is sterling when you hold it in your hand and it feels warm to the touch. Sterling silver consists of 925/1000 parts pure.

Silver

is the term used for plated items.

Hallmark

is the marking on silver which identifies the purity of silver or gold. The British hallmark usually displays a lion.

Holloware

Pieces of silver are light because they are hollow. Sometimes tar, pitch or plaster was filled in to give weight and strength to a candlestick or knife handle, This practice was used around the middle of the 19th century as a cost-cutting measure, since silver was highly taxed and the price of a solid silver item was astronomical.

Chasing

is the raised or relief pattern created on the surface of silver. Unlike engraving where silver is removed, silver is added.

Electroplate

Silver is fused to a base metal with a process involving an electrical current. If it is marked with **EPNS,** *(Electroplated Nickel Silver)* it means nickel base, silver plate on top. Thickness of plating determines quality. Most companies use 4 microns silver. Birks Regency plate is 10 microns thick which is the best quality.

EPBN

Electroplated Britannia Metal. This metal will have a dull *thud* when tapped. It is softer, and dents easier than other metals.

EPCN

Electroplated Copper / Nickel amalgam

Brian Says:

Most people assume that silver plated cutlery (community plate, Wm. Rogers) is of no great value. Not true. Depending on the pattern and quality, many collectors seek out wonderful old plated items. Plating extends into serving pieces such as entrée dishes and platters. The value depends on the quality and utility of each individual piece. (e.g: soup ladle)

As a rule, sterling items are four - five times more valuable than plated items.

Cleaning Tip

cleaning tip

Silver pieces should be washed as soon after use as possible since prolonged contact with food (especially acidic foods or eggs) will tarnish. Use a silver cleaner, NEVER bleach. Unfortunately, good intentions to create a shiny piece often results in silver being removed and exposing the metal underneath. When in doubt, ask an expert about cleaning and about re-silvering older pieces.

Gold Plate should not tarnish but benefits from a cleaning with a quality jewelry cleaner.

Cutlery with handles made from bone, ivory, horn, or wood are best kept out of water because it can cause the materials to split. The best way to wash these items is to stand them up in a container of warm (not hot) water and mild detergent. Remove the food, then wipe the handles clean.

Valuing Silver Pieces

The value of a piece is determined by age, pattern and by its function. The more specific the function, the higher the value. For example, a fork has greater value than a knife, and a soup ladle (only one would be found in a set) has greater value than a fork.

◄This set of sterling silver fruit spoons and sugar spoon are intricately decorated, and housed in a custom case. Not only is this set functional but beautiful and of excellent quality.

Storing and Displaying Silver

The tendency is to polish silver then protect it in plastic wrap to prevent further tarnish. Not a good idea. The silver will be damaged from the plastic wrap. Leave it uncovered, or keep it in a silver storage box, lined with silver cloth, and put in a block or two of camphor. If you are close to major industries, your silver will tarnish quickly. Store in airtight cases which slows the tarnishing process.

China/Porcelain

The process for creating fine porcelain was developed in China, and practically everything dealing with dishes is called *china*. However, there are other materials used. Porcelain, bone china, stoneware, ironstone are just some of the terms used to identify the materials used to make dinnerware, pottery and figurines.

While names like *Limoges* or *Belleek* are widely recognized, there is value to be found in china from other manufacturers. There are hundreds of manufacturers, many of which have undergone name changes as a result of mergers, sell outs and other changes. For example, some factories gained prestige after receiving a special order from a royal house, giving them the right to incorporate the name *Royal* into their company name.

When a china pattern is retired or no longer available, it does not automatically increase or decrease in value. A value will be placed on a piece according to the *last retail price* the last time it was available. Value will also be determined by condition, quality, and popularity. For example, Royal Winton Chintz is not of the highest quality, but is highly prized by collectors. On the other hand, if it was a quality piece at the time of purchase it's still quality. Function of a piece also affects value. A lunch plate will be considerably less than a covered soup tureen because a set of dishes will have only one tureen and many plates. A tureen with its original lid is more valuable than one without a lid. Even though great attempts are made to find a replacement lid, the fit is never quite perfect and the value is not as high as the original set.

Limoges

The name suggests quality and good taste, but in fact, that is not always the case. There are over 400 factories in the LIMOGES region of France, 200 Km. outside Paris. Factors affecting the value of Limoges are: artist, age of the piece, and condition. Consult an expert to be sure. American Limoges is not as highly prized as the French product.

Limoges lidded vegetable dish with original lid, finial, handles and legs beautifully intact.

Things to know about dishes

If there is no mark on the china, it is likely pre-1891. The McKinley Tariff Act required that the country of origin be marked on all china and porcelain.

Bone China

is bone ash mixed with clay to produce hard white china. The process developed about 1800, is still in use.

Hand-painted

The design is painted directly onto the dish by the artist. No two dishes are exactly alike. Dish-painting was a popular home hobby for young ladies during 1880-1910 when the artwork was applied to pieces called blanks.

▲ Adderley Bone China, Lowestoft

Made in Occupied Japan

1945-1952. During this time, Allies occupied Japan, and this marking appeared on all exported goods.

▲ Noritake Dish

Nippon

This was used as a country name (Japan) during 1891 - 1921, and later as a company name. After that time, *Made in Japan* or *Japan* was stamped on the bottom of china and porcelain.

Royal

Appears as part of the name of many English bone china manufacturers because they have created pieces for royalty.

22 Carat

This term was used after 1930's to identify real 22 carat gold. Anything with gold trim is definitely not dishwasher or microwave safe.

▲ Royal Cauldron Bean Pot

Majolica

is highly collectible pottery, often featuring animals, plants and fruit or insects and reptiles in a high relief design. Most majolica is made in Italy, England, Germany and France. Caution: this style is being widely copied today.

▲ Majolica 7" Coffee Pot
Valued over $1000

Underglaze

Design is applied, then glaze is applied over top making the design under the glaze.

Reticulated

Cutwork design done in porcelain.

Gilt

Gold or silver applied to edges and to highlight detail does add to overall value. Gold, silver or platinum is also applied to better quality items.

▲ Aynsley bone china cup and saucer, green with gold gilt design. Next to blue and white, pink is the most desirable colour.

Finial

The knob on lids that rarely escapes chipping or damage.

Transfer ware

The design is created on a thin tissue which is then adhered to the china. It is then hand decorated with a bit of colour, possibly air brushed then trimmed with gold.

▲ Royal Crown Derby, Blue Mikado sugar bowl. Notice the ornate final and handles.

Stoneware

fired at high temperatures to make the product imperious to liquids. It's seldom translucent, rarely white and much heavier than bone china and porcelain. Most often used as the everyday set.

Ironstone

is hard, durable earthenware patented in 1813 by Charles Mason. Early pieces are very expensive. Pieces may surface bearing the names of *Staffordshire, Davenport, Spode, Ridgeway,* and *Ashworth Brothers.*

▲ Covered cheese or butter dish, Woods & Sons dinner plate.

Cream ware

lightweight, whitish creamy English earthenware originally developed around 1740. *Wedgewood* and *Leeds* were leaders in creating cream ware and continue to create desirable pieces today.

Porcelain and China Backstamps

Attempting to follow the family tree of a porcelain manufacturer or a bone china manufacturer can be a confusing and frustrating , especially since many companies were subdivided within families, renamed, sold, resold and renamed again.

The backstamps which follow, (page 57 - 59) are examples of some of the better quality bone china and porcelain factories. Look for these when sorting through vases, figurines, decorative dishes, plates and platters and china. Many reference books give greater detail about markings with dates and colours to help you determine the age of a piece.

Don't be confused by the lack of a mark on china or porcelain and immediately conclude it is older than 1891. Many new pieces, made to look old, are currently being mass produced and marked with paper labels which easily fall off. Be especially aware of this when rummaging through garage sales and flea markets.

David McBirney
& Co. (Beleek
Pottery Co.)

W. Moorcroft
Ltd.Burslem,
Staffordshire, Eng.

British Anchor Pottery
Co. Ltd.

Reinhold
Schlegelmilch (R.S.
Prussia) 1869-1938

Crown Derby
Porcelain, Derby
England (Royal
Doulton Tableware
Ltd.)

Worcester Royal
Porcelain Co.
Ltd. , England

KAISER PORCELAIN
Staffelstein, Bavaria,

ENGLAND

ENGLAND

Villeroy & Boch,
Mettlach

LENOX

Lenox Inc. Trenton N.J.
Hardpaste porcelain

Wood & Sons Ltd.
Burslem & Stoke,
Staffordshire,
England 1865 -
present

WEDGWOOD

ENGLAND

Philip Rosenthal & Co.,
Bavaria Germany

Minton

Blue and White

Blue and white designs on china have been popular since the Ming Dynasty when it was discovered that cobalt could be used to create a brilliant blue in the glaze. Factories and artists have copied and adapted the patterns and styles of other artists, creating a huge choice for collectors, and a huge headache for appraisers! The most desirable patterns are

▲ Blue Willow Platter

those depicting a scene, such as in a Blue Willow pattern. Much of the blue and white china found now is English, and is created with a transfer ware process which makes designs consistent and easy to produce in large quantity.

Coffee pot or Chocolate pot?

At one time, chocolate was regarded as *the* fashionable beverage of choice, and was served in pots made specifically for that exotic beverage. The lid was often hinged, to allow for a quick stir before serving. The bottom of the chocolate pot was bulbous, enabling a really good stir. The spout of the chocolate

pot (right) is higher, and wide enough to allow for a spoon to be inserted, without having to remove the lid. Chocolate pots are highly collectible.

The spout of the coffee pot (left) is low and there is always a multi-holed strainer at the base of the spout to strain out the coffee grounds.

◄ Stunning Limoges chocolate pot from turn of the century. Hand painted with delicate pink and green foliage and trimmed with gold. Some of the design is raised making it beautiful to the touch as well as to the eye.
Value: $750

▲ 1930's walnut veneer buffet. In addition to storing china and linens, it is also useful as a display surface for special pieces of silver and china. Interestingly enough, mothers are often faced with the problem of *who gets the candlesticks*, and wishing to avoid conflict amongst the children, splits the set. This also happens with crystal, figurines, vases and many other items meant to be kept as pairs or sets. Unfortunately, splitting items decreases value by as much as 75 - 90%.

▲ Walnut veneer dining room table from 1929. Extensions slide out from either end making the table suitable for six or more to dine.

▶Mahogany veneer host chair or arm chair from 1926.

▼Mahogany veneer side chair from 1930. Both styles would have been included as part of the dining room set which likely had five more dining chairs. Seat covering was either brocade or leather. In the 40's, the leather changed to leatherette which was an early attempt to produce a leather-like fabric. Often, the seats were recovered with handmade needlepoint .

▶The perfect place to store beautiful china when not in use: the china cabinet. This mahogany veneer cabinet is typical of those found in the 1930's and held china as well as linens. Some had specially lined drawers for silver flatware. Reproductions exist and modern pieces are often fitted with plastic pegs for adjustable shelving. Replace these with metal ones right away because plastic ones break and the cost of replacing the fine china and crystal is not worth the risk.

Value: $1000 - $1500

The
Kitchen

The kitchen is the heart of the home, the central traffic area, the catch-all place for everything from bread tags and keys to mittens, mail, homework and soup cans.

In many homes, the kitchen is the heart-beat of the family. It is where families gather for meals, recap events of the day, prepare for family events or just hang out and raid the refrigerator for a snack.

Technology and fast foods may have changed the way we use the kitchen, and its function as a gathering place may not be as common as it once was, but it is still the room that manages to accumulate an odd assortment of stuff. Be prepared to spend lots of time sorting through this room. The little things here can be overwhelming.

Wedgewood Stove, from the early 40's is still in perfect working order. With two ovens, and two broiler elements, four top burners and a grill, just looking at it, one can imagine the smell of the Sunday dinner that's cooking!

Kitchen	Keep	Sell	Bequest
Appliances			
Gadgets			
Dishes			
Everyday			
China			
Porcelain			
Serving			
Pieces			

Kitchen	Keep	Sell	Bequest
Glassware			
Bake ware			
Collectibles			
Wall			
Decorations			
Furniture			

A Freezer Story

When Mrs. Peters passed away, she was in her 90's and had been in the same home for more than fifty years. Everyone applauded the feisty lady for her independence and ability to maintain her own home. Her daughters took turns coming at different times throughout the year to assist with the 'big' housecleaning, but mostly, Mrs. Peters did everything herself.

When the time came for the final cleaning, the daughters shared the task. It was when they tackled the deep-freezer, that they began to question the quality of their mother's independence. They found packages of meat that were beyond recognition. How long the meat had been in the freezer was anyone's guess. They began to wonder if the electricity had ever failed. Had things thawed and been frozen again? Who knew? Everything had to be discarded, an act that would have horrified Mrs. Peters who had survived the depression years by being frugal, keeping and using everything rather than being wasteful.

Mrs. Peter's story is typical of her generation. Without intending to, health hazards may have been created by trying to save money and keep things on hand. How healthy is your grandmother's home?

Vintage red paint Fairbury Windmill water pump; the original indoor plumbing. Value: decorative but as high as $60.

About Salt

At one time, salt was placed in a great salt, or a dish just for salt. It was an important and precious commodity because it used to preserve meat and was, therefore, offered sparingly at the table. Salt on the table suggested the host was wealthy, and elaborate salt cellars were eventually crafted for serving.

·Elaborately decorated sterling silver salt cellar, glass liner, no spoon.

In ancient Rome, it was used to pay the soldiers of Imperial Rome! The word salary is derived from sal which is Latin word for salt. A good soldier then, was 'worth his salt'.

Cleaning the Kitchen

Step one: get a large supply of garbage bags.

Step two: get a large supply of rubber gloves.

Step three: start dumping: food items, elastic bands, bread tags, twist tags, opened bottles of spices, herbs, plastic bags, plastic

Condiment set, Made In Japan

containers, plastic cutlery, paper napkins, magazine clippings, coupons, toothpicks. tinfoil pans.

Step four: sort cupboards according to function: dishes, pots and pans, electrical appliances, cutlery, baking pans, recipe books, glassware, ornaments.

Step five: Step back and decide what else to toss, give, keep and appraise!!

Glassware

In the same way that manufacturers are reproducing bone china patterns and pieces, they are also reproducing glassware. Beware.

▲ Depression era open lace plate, pink glass, early 1900's. Value: $60

Depression glass

This glassware has a definable pattern name, loosely attributed to the period between 1920 -1950. It was mass produced in a variety of patterns, colours and for various uses from perfume bottles to serving dishes. This glassware added a bright note to the depression era. It was available through mail order catalogues, or often given away at food stores, gas stations and even for special nights, such as *plate night*, at the movies! The fewer pieces of a particular pattern and color that were made, the greater the value.

Carnival Glass

▲ Carnival Glass compote Value: $65

Pieces made of iridescent glass, and so named because they were frequently given away at carnivals as prizes. Carnival glass was made in America in 1929 as an inexpensive substitute for higher quality glass. Quite collectible, it is also being reproduced. White opalescent, aqua, peach, ice blue and smoke are the most popular and desirable colours of carnival glass. To see the true colour, hold the piece up to the light. The colour will be revealed by looking through the centre of the base.

▲ Reproduction Blue Glass Footed Dish

Milk Glass

This white milky glass was originally called Opalware and was made in England. If you can see through it, it isn't milk glass. It was also produced in France and USA during the latter part of the century. New milk glass is inferior to Opalware. There are many reproductions made today with the Fenton backstamp. Don't be fooled. Names worth watching for: *Fenton, McKee,* and *Westmoreland.*

▲ Westmoreland footed fruit dish with reticulated edging

Jadeite

▼ Jadeite Skillet

This pretty glass is green or sometimes blue. Coffee cups can be found everywhere, it seems, but the more unusual pieces, such as canisters, gravy boats and patterned fruit dishes are sought after. Practically everything was made in this glass, from ovenware to tableware, decorative pieces such as vases, and utility pieces such as rolling pins and juice reamers.

Fiesta Ware

is being produced once again. It is best to consult an expert to determine authenticity of pieces considered to be old. Initially, it was popular for the bright colours and inexpensive price tag. Old pieces are collectible but reproductions have driven prices of the original down. Why buy high priced old when you can get the brand new pieces for much less? Caution: the old orange Fiesta Ware pieces were LEAD based and are highly toxic. Keep these for display rather than for food storage and serving.

▲ New Fiesta pitcher, sunflower yellow colour. Value: $23 US

▲ Blown glass bud vases.

Blown Glass

Blown glass is created by blowing through a tube and shaping glass with quick turns then cutting with specialized tools. The process requires skilled hands and quick movements to shape and create a perfect piece. Colours are added in the blowing process and sometimes bubbles are added to create greater interest. Blown glass pieces have very fluid lines and are more decorative than functional. Don't be misled by raw *ponteil** marks on the base. (*the place where the item sits on a base when fired) These could also be reproductions.

▲ Pressed glass plate
Value: $250

Pressed Glass

Pressed glass is created by pouring molten glass into a mold, and pressing. The pattern is consistent, and feels smooth to the touch. Edges of pressed glass are rounded and smooth.

Cut Glass

Incisions are cut into glass with special tools, creating edges that catch the light and make the glass sparkle. Edges are sharper to the touch and more defined than pressed glass. Cut glass is fragile and easily damaged, and must be handled with care. It is labour intensive to create, expensive to buy, and at one time was the gift of choice for newlyweds. While pieces such as stemware may look identical, there may be small differences because each piece is hand done. New cut glass designs are done with lasers and the edges are almost razor sharp and most often not as highly polished as earlier pieces.

▲ Cranberry cut glass vase Value: $350

Etching

Design technique used on glass. Acid is brushed through a design cut into a metal plate. An etched design has a frosty appearance and will be rough to the touch.

Hand Painted

Designs are painted onto the glass surface. Easy to distinguish between hand painting and transfer: the hand painting reveals brush strokes while poorly done transfer pieces often have wrinkles or inconsistencies in places where patterns should join up smoothly, such as vines and leaves.

Opalescent

This is glass with an iridescent look when placed in direct light. Most often, pink is the dominant colour that will be revealed, especially around the edges.

▲ Detail painted on green glass vase, likely by Mary Gregory.

▲ Late 1800's pink satin glass biscuit jar with silver lid. and handle. Value: $350 - $400

Brian says:

Many pieces and patterns of glassware are being reproduced in Japan and are surfacing in flea markets and garage sales as the genuine product. Determining authenticity can be confusing, so be careful. This is especially true of Depression era glass. Get a reference book and research the glass before you go in search of pieces for your collection. Look for obvious wear on the bottom of all pieces to determine if it is old. New pieces will have no wear at all.

Kitchen Gadgets

How many ways can you beat an egg? How many ways can you cut vegetables? meat? bread? Seems there are more ways than one can imagine. The following are examples of some of the tools designed to make life easier for the happy homemaker at the turn of the century. Don't be fooled into thinking they are worthless!

◄Egg beaters were not only for beating eggs! Cakes, creams, puddings were lighter and fluffier after using any of the dozens of variations of egg beaters. These examples are from 1908, and have names like *Cyclone* and *Light Running*. Before tossing any of these out, consult an appraiser. The values, though not great, may actually surprise you.

◄Chopping knives made of stainless steel and painted wooden handles. Useful in the kitchen of 1925.

▲Pre-electric dough mixer. One had to hold the mixer in the crook of the arm, and literally put their back into getting the crank to turn.

►Chopping blades, from 1900 made of wood and iron.

Tableware

To ease confusion, we have kept all the china and porcelain markings in the dining room section. However, there is still something to be said about tableware that was created for the mass market. Ideally, tableware was designed to be affordable and functional, yet still attractive for everyday dining.

Pieces by *Shelley, Susie Cooper, Carlton, Royal Winton* (especially the Chintz patterns) from the 1930 - 60's have increased dramatically in value. As pieces were used on a daily basis, they got cracked and chipped and eventually were discarded. However, some pieces remained intact and are of great interest to people wanting to complete a collection of a particular pattern. The most difficult and expensive pieces to find are items like teapots (with original lid) or lidded serving bowls since only one of these came with a set and fewer were made.

▲ Set of Pyrex Mixing bowls were useful for mixing, baking and serving. Finding a complete set that hasn't been scratched, chipped or broken is difficult, and this $10 garage sale find is worth almost six times what the new owner paid.

You won't find *Tiffany* or *Lalique* in the kitchen, but you will find refrigerator jars made by *Federal, Pyrex* and *Fireking.*

▲ Red Pyrex lidded refrigerator dish often came in a set with varying sizes and in primary colours.

These colourful containers with the heavy glass lids were also safe for use in the oven, a bonus for the modern home-maker of 1950's. Many patterns and designs evolved and collectors are interested in specific patterns and colours, and component parts to complete their sets.

►Sometimes, the best things in life *are* free, and these examples of a cream, sugar and cereal bowl are no exception. Pieces came in specially marked packages of flour, and entire sets could be collected, providing you did lots of baking! Plates were easy to collect but the more difficult pieces were the serving pieces such as cream and sugar, covered vegetable dishes, and platters. This set of green and cream coloured Colonial Homestead was popular in the early 1950's with each piece depicting a different aspect of pioneer life.

◄Brushed aluminum canisters from the early 1950's were also popular in a well appointed kitchen. Stainless steel look is all the rage now, and pieces like these are quite desirable! Value: $35

►To keep up with Mom, and practice household skills, children were given their own set of graniteware pots and pans. This child's toy set of a graniteware wash set is rare and valued at over $230 US.

Milk Glass

White Crystal was most popular between 1895 -1910. Made into everything from perfume bottles and vases, to cake plates and complete table settings, it is quite collectible. *Fenton, Westmoreland,* and *Imperial* are best known for creating these treasures. Hobnail patterns first appeared in the 1920's, and again in the '50's when Fenton expanded the design to other pieces.

▲FireKing milk glass in the very popular hobnail pattern

◄The kitchen of the 1920's usually had one of these: a Hoosier cabinet. With tin lined drawers and bins, it was useful for storing sugar, flour, (notice the spout for dispensing flour) and other essential baking ingredients. Drawers stored baking utensils and the surface, covered in porcelain or tin, made dough rolling a pleasure. Out of fashion for a time, these are once again of interest. Values can be as high as $2500, depending on craftsmanship and condition.

Furniture

Kitchen furniture usually consisted of table, chairs, stools, or benches (for really big families). Tables, like this one from 1920 was useful because it could be quickly expanded, or tucked away against the wall when

not in use. Some tables had porcelain or tin tops, doubling as a baking preparation surface. Others had drawers underneath for additional storage. Many kitchen tables and cupboards ended up painted and covered with decals.

Drop-leaf oak table, 1920.

It is important to remember not to attempt to repair or restore any piece until it has first been appraised and evaluated. Repairs require expert attention from a select group of craftsmen. Water spots and scratches can be removed and broken

legs and damaged knobs replaced. Peeling and chipped veneer can also be repaired, thereby restoring a piece to its original glory.

▲Oak veneer extension table. This one divides in the middle, and the base splits. An extra leaf or two is added, making room for more to gather round the table. These tables were very popular in the 20's and 30's and, in good condition, are still quite desirable pieces because of the seating flexibility. Depending on craftsmanship, number of leaves and condition, value could reach as high as $2000.

Table coverings

Vintage tablecloths, linens, doilies, and napkins are fairly abundant. Usually, they are well worn, and may have signs of repeated use. Unless the piece has high sentimental value, restoration is likely not worth the effort.

To clean a piece on your own, first determine the kind of stain that you are dealing with, then proceed. For ordinary stains, soak the cloth in 100% AMAZE soap flakes and water overnight. For stains, make a paste from the soap flakes, and brush gently in four directions with a very soft brush such as a mushroom brush. Continue washing carefully by hand. Be sure to completely rinse all Amaze out of the fabric, then rewash with regular laundry soap. If you are unsure, check with the experts. Items with permanent stains or holes are not worth a great deal.

To store vintage linens, roll them around a tube, and wrap with archival tissue paper to prevent crease and fold damage.

Detail from a 1940's printed table cloth. These cloths, in pristine condition, are selling once again, to collectors interested in creating a retro decorating scheme.

Occasionally, pieces have historical value if they were owned or created by someone of historical importance. Provenance (documentation) in this case, is absolutely essential.

Vintage cloth is of interest to collectors, but only if the condition is pristine. Before tossing, do a little research. Occasionally, vintage cloths are in demand.

Valuing Textiles

Many hours are spent creating beautiful table linens, aprons, tea towels, guest towels, bed linens and doilies. Embroidery, crocheting and knitting are skills required by any young girl who wished to fill the hope chest which would one day supply her with all that she needed for her own holiday tables.

These heirloom treasures are usually handed down to daughters and carefully folded and tucked into the closet. Unfortunately, folding creates nasty creases causing the fabric to break on the folds. Vintage linens can be restored, but first consider the sentimental value and the monetary value.

Generally, the more handwork that has been done, the greater the value placed on the piece. Detail, and quality of work affect the value. However, while the handwork that Grandma created to adorn a chair may

beautify the chair, it does not increase or add to the value of a good antique. If pieces are in pristine condition, collectors will pay higher prices for pieces to add to their collection.

▲Table runner from 1940's, hand embroidered.

◄Embroidered pillow case with crocheted edging; hand work such as this helped pass many long winter evenings.

The Bedroom

What a great place to hide treasures! Usually, that's where Grandmother hid her treasures; in drawers, in boxes in back of the closet, under the bed, and in little pouches tucked under linens in trunks. It might also be the room that doubled as a sewing room when it wasn't a guest room, or an extra sitting room. There is likely much more here than meets the eye.

	Bedroom	Keep	Sell	Bequest
Furniture				
Rugs				
Collectibles				
Jewelry				
Radio				
Television				

Bedroom	Keep	Sell	Bequest
Pictures			
Paintings			
Tapestries			
Posters			
Heirloom			
Textiles			
Quilts			
Vintage clothes			
designer clothing			
Furs			
Sewing Goods			

Vintage Bed Linens

Unless bed linens are heirloom, hold sentimental value or are of artist quality, they are valuable only as used bed linens. Quilt collectors and vintage lace collectors may be interested in handcrafted quilts, bedspreads, pillowcases and cushions. The only exceptions are real 100% linen bedclothes.

If the bedroom also functioned as a sewing room, then sewing notions, fabrics and so on may also have value to people collecting vintage quality. Before tossing, sort through carefully. Even packages are of value to those collecting vintage notions. The wrapper for a package of needles confirms the age of the product, and adds to the value. The value, however, is not great. Some items are desired for decoration more than function.

▲ Close-up detail from vintage hand sewn lace bedspread

◄ Antique ivory inlaid tatting shuttle

Jewelry

There is considerable interest in estate jewelry, particularly high quality jewelry. It is strongly advised that quality jewelry be properly appraised by an accredited jewelry appraiser. Attempts to be thrifty at this point will cost you in the long run. Take suspected precious metal items to a jeweler who agrees to appraise while you wait. No appraiser should ever suggest keeping the jewelry or sending it away. There is no reason to have to send things away to be appraised.

Victorian pin in gold with amethyst and seed pearls.

You will be given a certificate for each item, which states the quality of any gems and precious metals, as well as an indication of age, condition and value. The appraisal should also reflect the current value of gold and silver per ounce, plus weight in ounces of that item. If the item has diamonds, quality and colour grading will also be included. Without such a certificate, buyers may be less tempted to pay a reasonable price for the jewelry.

Sterling Silver Thistle pin, shows a hallmark on the back.

▲ Engraved initials

▲ Hallmark on watch back identifies maker and gold content.

▲ 1920 Nickel Watch with unique expandable clasp.
Value: $350

Estate Jewelry

is jewelry that is second hand, previously enjoyed, loved and left. It need not be antique to be estate, and need not be precious to be considered estate jewelry. Each piece has a unique history, and tells the story of the fashion of the day, and the technology and skills of the time that inspired the jeweler's art.

Precious Metal Jewelry

Look for hallmarks such as .800 which means it is 800 parts out of 1000 pure or .925/1000. Hallmarks, like those found on sterling silver and gold pieces reflect the makers mark and the quality of the piece. Engraved pieces are personalized and have nothing to do with the value of the piece. This engraving can quite likely be removed.

Costume Jewelry

If there is a name or a marking on the back, then look closer. Don't sell it until it has been appraised and you know what it's really worth. Look for names like *Coro, Dior, Trifari, Swarovski, Sherman,* and *Tiffany* on the back of jewelry. Remember rhinestones? They're back in style. However, value drops dramatically if stones are missing.

▶The safety clasp was patented in 1849 but didn't really *catch* on until 1911. Prior to that time, a simple, insecure C-clasp was used.

◀This precious antique enamel bug pin is created with pearls, and diamonds. Antique jewelry with pearls is very collectible.

◀Vintage clothing, like this pair of shoes from the 1930's, is of interest to consignment stores specializing in vintage clothes. Generally, if the item was quality new, it is quality now, provided it is in pristine condition.

◀If there's a really silly tie out there, chances are you gave it to your dad, or someone else did, and now you are finding it and a zillion others in the closet. Unless the tie is a designer label, signed and in pristine condition, it isn't worth much. If Dad was gracious enough to allow himself to be photographed wearing your gift, frame it along with the tie, and enjoy the memory.

A Sisters Story

Recently, Brian encountered two sisters who had inherited more than forty pieces of jewelry. He encouraged them to take the pieces for appraisal before attempting to dispose of anything. Two of the pieces in the collection were appraised at $11,000 and $12,000. The cost for this appraisal? $30. What's the appraisal worth? Priceless!

◄Sterling Silver dresser set includes: mirror, brush, comb, pin box and clothing brush in custom box. If this was Birks sterling, replacement cost would be $1500 or more.

►Limoges wash basin and pitcher. Now purely decorative, these were once standard items found in almost every bedroom.

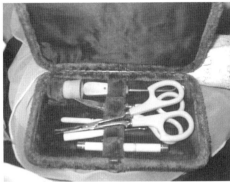

◄One never traveled anywhere without a sewing set in their possession. This example includes two ivory handled scissors, needle case, thimble, and hook .

►Beaded handbag big enough for lipstick, a handkerchief and a dance card. These bags range in value from $50 - $350.

▼Bone carved needle case Value: $175

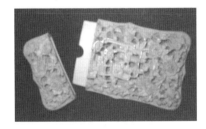

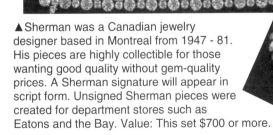

▲Sherman was a Canadian jewelry designer based in Montreal from 1947 - 81. His pieces are highly collectible for those wanting good quality without gem-quality prices. A Sherman signature will appear in script form. Unsigned Sherman pieces were created for department stores such as Eatons and the Bay. Value: This set $700 or more.

►Bureau and ▼vanity of walnut veneer, late 1930, are typical of pieces found in older estates. These two pieces have carved detail around the border, and brass handles and knobs. A full bedroom suite would also include a headboard and footboard.

►Zebrawood veneer vanity chair (named so because the stripes resemble a zebra's stripes). Late 1930's

▲Birdseye maple veneer washstand (also called a commode washstand), late 1930's. Value: $350 - $500.

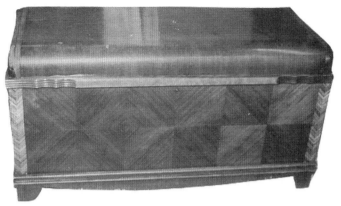

▲Walnut veneer cedar chest, late 1930's. Pieces such as this often were labeled as genuine walnut veneer to distinguish them from mass produced pieces using simulated walnut veneers, thus guaranteeing customers that they were paying for the genuine product.

▶Hand painted, satin lined, gold plated porcelain jewel box with hinged lid. American made, probably one-of-a-kind. Insurance value suggested: $1000.

▲Don't be too quick to toss out perfume bottles. This one, made in France was appraised at $450.

Additional Items	Keep	Sell	Bequest

The Kids Room

Depending on how long ago the kids left home, and what they took with them will determine whether or not these will be a pleasant rooms to tackle. Usually, when they leave, they take the good stuff with them leaving the rest for you. Sooner or later, however, they may come back to you and ask, '*Do you remember that toy I used to have when I was a kid? Where is it?*' When that happens, it's a safe bet they've discovered that some vintage toys have appreciated in value, such as the *Star Wars* dolls in this picture. Purchased at the time of the first movie, kept in their original boxes, and untouched, the dolls are valued from $200 - $800 each.

Kids Room	Keep	Sell	Bequest
Furniture			
Toys			
dolls			
games			
Books			
comics			
computers			
radios			
clocks			

Kids Room	Keep	Sell	Bequest
Collectibles			
Wall			
decorations			
autographed			
posters			
Personal			
awards			
papers			
photos			
memorabilia			
School Stuff			

William's Story

William and Ron's mother passed away suddenly, leaving them and their families with the overwhelming task of cleaning out her home of more than forty years.

Everyone wanted to get the job done quickly so that they could return to their families and routines. As they worked their way through room after room, drawer after drawer, they were not only confronted with their mother's collection of memories, but with their own as well. Shoeboxes crammed with school stuff; photographs and programs tucked into bookshelves; newspaper clippings sandwiched between the pages of books or tucked under the drawer linings. It was emotionally exhausting to stop and visit each memory. Soon indiscriminate tossing began.

One drawer revealed a collection of buttons and badges that had been earned and collected by William when he was a child. He paused long enough to tell the story of how hard he had worked to earn the badges but the thought of taking them from a drawer in his mom's house to a drawer in his own did not appeal to him, so the badges were tossed. His wife, however, saw an opportunity and discreetly rescued them from destruction. A few months later, on the occasion of William's 60th birthday, she gave him the badges; beautifully mounted and framed with a photo of William at the age he had begun the collection.

What's a drawer full of badges worth? Not much. What's a collection of badges, thoughtfully and lovingly preserved worth? Priceless.

1948 LMS model train engine

A Word about Toys

Toys that feature characters from television, movies or very popular children's stories are quite collectible. Condition, original boxes or packaging, and popularity of the character affect the price. Toys that were wildly popular are surprisingly still collectible: such as *Slinky, Nerf* ball, and decks of card games like *Old Maid*. Before you toss, consider that this is an area where your trash might definitely be someone else's treasure, and appraisal is required.

▲ Children's card games, featuring Disney and classic characters from the 60's and 70's.

Recently, a *Fisher Price* hospital set sold for $225 US. Remember those little plastic toys from MacDonald's that came with kids meals in the 80's? They can sell for $25 or more.

Other collectibles include lunch boxes, lamps, matchbox cars, trains, and jigsaw puzzles.

▲ Ronald Macdonald stuffed toy

▲ Nerf Ball! 1969

▲ Slinky 1960's

▲ The Easy Show Projector by Kenner, was a have-to-have in the late 60's. Finding one intact in a box, with all the slides is rare.

▲ 1976 Fisher Price Hospital

▲ This Emma doll is a true antique. With porcelain head and hands, kid leather knees and elbows, she is a treasure. Unfortunately, her original clothing has long since been replaced but she is still a valuable find. To display antique dolls, purchase a doll stand and a glass dome to keep off the dust. Value: $750 - $850

▲ Mattel's Mrs. Beasley made famous on the 1967 television show: *Family Affair*

Dolls

At one time, Barbie dolls fetched a large sums. However, these dolls are becoming less rare and less valuable. The doll market goes in cycles, largely depending on the age of the collector. For example, few collectors younger than forty would be interested in finding a Shirley Temple doll for their collection.

The Office or Library

Most homes have a desk and a collection of papers, books, maps, and photos. The popularity of the in-home office means computers, disks, printers, fax machines, CD's and high tech related equipment and accessories are part of the home inventory.

The library will also include encyclopedias, pens, paperweights, lamps, letter openers, stamps, personal letters and possibly unusual office equipment and accessories.

Antique
Kneehole desk

Sorting through this collection will require considerable time and concentration. First of all, the personal items need to be separated from the ordinary, and the extraordinary from the clutter.

Office	Keep	Sell	Bequest
Lamps			
Fixtures			
Office			
Equipment			
and			
Furniture			
Pictures			
Paintings			

Office	Keep	Sell	Bequest
Clocks			
Stereo			
Television			
CD, tapes recordings			
Collections			
Vases			
Planters			
and			
Decorative			
Carpets			
Rugs			

Make a separate listing for all books and printed materials such as maps, charts, which have collectible value. Do the same with recordings, videos, CD's and other sound recordings.

Katherine's story

My parents owned and operated a general store where I spent much of my pre-school days. One of my favourite places was Dad's office, especially when he would be writing in his big ledger. Long columns of numbers and long lists were beautifully written in black ink with pens that I loved to touch. He only used the pens for the ledger and of course, I was not encouraged to touch them! He would, however, give me paper and other pens and pencils and I would try to make numbers and letters look like his. Time passed quietly, with him scratching away and me scribbling. I loved those moments. It was there that he taught me to create a unique signature. It was there that he taught me to count money. I still have his pens, and when I hold one in my hand, I am taken right back to those happy times spent with Dad in his office.

Walking through the Office

The office will be the place where you will find photographs, documents, warranties and manuals, letters and postcards, greeting cards and concert programs. You will find computer disks, keys, video cassettes and slides, recordings and tapes, CDs and an ocean of paper and a ton of books. This is probably the most personal room in the whole house because it also stores the written and visual history of the family.

Since many retired professionals maintain a home office, you will likely find books and documents that are specifically related to their field of expertise.

Some of the items may be valuable to the family, while others may be of historical interest to a local or provincial museum, or archive relating to that person's career. Because of the sensitive nature of much of the material in this room, it may be necessary to destroy some papers to protect personal information and privacy. Get a paper shredder if you don't already have one. However, consult with family members before making this kind of decision. Do not remove redundant paperwork without checking. Repercussions could be costly.

Office Equipment

Many seniors have hooked up to high speed internet service and purchased computers, printers, scanners and digital camera equipment to keep up with family email and photo exchanges. According to Stats Canada 1996, 25% of the households, headed by a senior, own a computer. That number is increasing significantly as the population ages and brings their technology with them. Before disposing of computer equipment,

1940's Oak desk chair, swivel, height adjusted by adding or subtracting wooden disks.

be sure that all personal files have been completely erased. If unsure how to do this, check with a reputable computer consultant. Save important files to disks and then sell or give away the equipment. If the equipment is completely obsolete, contact your local disposal company. There are environmentally sound ways to dispose of computers and electronic equipment.

Carpets, Rugs

Generally, most carpets and rugs should be pulled out, destroyed and replaced, especially if the home is going to be sold. Occasionally, a carpet will be valuable, such as a Persian rug, or a Native / Aboriginal rug. An expert should be consulted before deciding what to do with those.

Books

Regardless of whether the author is alive or dead, books hold or increase in value depending on the success of the book, and whether or not it is a first edition. For example, a first edition Beatrix Potter is very desirable, as is a Harry Potter first title, first edition, or a Stephen King novel. Book club editions of books are valueless so they can be donated. Generally, encyclopedias and reference books don't hold value unless the picture plates of maps flowers, scenes and so forth are unique and considered works of art. Paperback books can be given away or tossed. Don't save old newspapers. Most of them are in poor condition and cannot be preserved. (see the Toss-It list, page 23)

Photo Albums, Video and Camera equipment

Most slides fade after twenty or more years making them virtually impossible to view clearly. Sort through them, selecting the best, then have them digitally converted to disk. For an additional cost, text and / or audio may be added. Make duplicate copies for other family members. The results will be priceless. Old colour photographs also have a tendency to fade, and new technology makes restoration a fairly easy process. Again, sort, select and duplicate for other family members. The result will be a priceless family history.

Bronze horse bookends. The combination of bronze and horses makes this set quite desirable.

Photographic equipment varies in value depending on age, original quality, and uniqueness of the technology and so on. Chemicals need to be disposed of safely. Contact the fire department for instructions.

Most Kodak type cameras are not of value. The same is true of old movie cameras. Do, however, have a second look at bellows-type cameras that fold-up like an accordion. Always check the camera for unexposed film. A client of Brian's found a camera with undeveloped film which, when processed, revealed a photo of a famous film star! The photo alone is priceless. Not bad for fifty year old film!

Furniture, lamps

Recently, Brian appraised an unusual chair from the 1950's. The chair was black leather stretched over a laminated plywood frame on a stainless steel base. Made by Fritz Hansen and designed by Arne Jacobsen, the chair's replacement value was determined to be $5000. The chair was originally used as a salesman sample for twenty-five years, and bought at a garage sale for $175.

Desk Sets

Some desk sets are real treasures. The materials used such as: leather, metals, wood, or semi-precious

▲ This exquisite Italian marble inkwell with brass detailed edging and colourful inlaid enamel, belongs to a time before email, when penmanship and the art of writing letters was greatly valued. Value: $400 - $500

▲ 1950's Forestville Clock, with solid brass pendulum, chimes on the hour and half hour.

▲ This unusual brass clock, in the shape of a horseshoe, was won in a horserace in the early 1800's. Owners are still seeking information regarding Queen Victoria's involvement in the presentation of this trophy.

stone, condition and design affects value and desirability.

Clocks

Clock repairmen are few and far between. Before deciding to repair an antique clock, get at least two written estimates. INSIST on authentic, not homemade parts, and be sure to get a warranty for all repairs.

Clocks must sit perfectly level to function. Use a level; front to back, left to right, then don't move it; simply open the face to wind it. Most clocks have a eight day wind cycle. By winding it every seven days, one day is reserved. Therefore, most clocks were wound on the Sabbath.

Pocket watches, which are found in nearly every home, should be brought to the attention of a qualified jeweler.

▶Desks come in many sizes and styles. This desk, called a high top secretary, made with tiger maple veneer, would be quite at home in a living room or dining room. The top has ample room for treasured tomes, while the drop leaf section hides a writing surface and pigeon holes for papers. The drawers have ample room for albums and files. Shelves without grooves are meant for books. Made in the late 1930's.

◀Drop-lid oak desk from 1920, was affordable and is of a style commonly found in many estates today. Lots of pigeon-holes inside for envelopes and papers, and usually drawers with dividers for pens, inks, stamps and other paraphernalia. Drawers inside the drop-leaf section were sometimes lined with felt. Drawers on the bottom had ample room for larger files, or even linens.

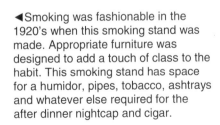

◀Smoking was fashionable in the 1920's when this smoking stand was made. Appropriate furniture was designed to add a touch of class to the habit. This smoking stand has space for a humidor, pipes, tobacco, ashtrays and whatever else required for the after dinner nightcap and cigar.

▲Waterfall front, Asian veneer knee-hole desk, 1930's. Lots of room for paper and file storage.

▲Library Desk or table with veneer top. Made in the 1920's. Shelves underneath provide room for book storage.

Mahogany furniture was very popular during the 1920'a and 30's. Sometimes less expensive furniture was stained to appear mahogany which caused confusion and frustration for buyers wanting the genuine article. Consequently, furniture was later labeled 'genuine mahogany'. These labels are sometimes found underneath tables, inside drawers and on the underside of chairs.

Paperweights

Paperweights come in all kinds of materials, from glass and porcelain (for example, hollow animal figures with a rubber stopper underneath are meant to be filled with sand or beans and used as a paperweight) to metals such as brass, and carved stone.

Glass paperweights are beautiful when held up to the light. These are quite desirable and some are very valuable. CAUTION: The tendency is to display these glass pieces in a window, usually placed on a piece of furniture, to catch the light. The problem is, the sun going through the glass on a very hot day can create serious damage to the furniture. Either close the drapes, or put the glass elsewhere to eliminate the danger of costly damage. Light stands may be purchased which are designed specifically to illuminate glass items.

Coins and Stamps

Collecting stamps and coins is a great way for children to learn world history and geography, and many have filled albums with samples purchased for that purpose. Unfortunately, fun and some education is often the greatest value for these collections.

The majority of coins and stamps kept for investment reasons have very little value. Coins that have been sold as good investments through the Royal Canadian mint are at best, only worth their face value. Some Olympic 1988 coin sets that sold for $450 are now worth less than $225. Some Olympic sets which sold for $375 have now been declared 'not for legal tender'. Truly valuable coins are already in the possession of serious, private collectors and are well insured and stored.

Stamps torn off letters are rarely valuable and the same holds true for corner dot sets. Consult a reference such as: *Charlton Guide to Coins and Stamps*, if in doubt. Serious philatelists know who owns the really rare and valuable stamps, and theirs is an elite club.

War Souvenirs, memorabilia

Unfortunately, those who still remember the war are aging and disappearing. Their medals are often tucked away and rarely, if ever, seen. The stories about the medals are fading and the value of the memorabilia is diminishing. Some military museums are interested in complete collections: photos, documents, uniforms, medals, and so forth as they tell the entire story of the original owner. Unless the family really values these items and wishes to keep them intact, the museum may be the best place to preserve the stories of our war heroes. A donation to a recognized museum is considered a donation to the queen and a 100% tax credit may be allowed. Check for these details.

Preserve photos and medals in frames and display them proudly. This is a part of family history that should be treasured.

Embroidered Postcard

TRENCH ART (items made by POW's) are sought after by collectors because they are unique. Ships in bottles, artillery casings converted into vases and lighters from bullets are just some of the items you might find wrapped in the folds of an old pair of socks next to the medals.

The Garage

◄Imagine riding around on this antique cast iron Hoosier farm implement seat.
You may find one rusting somewhere in the barn. Even if it isn't a Hoosier, it is still surprisingly valuable, and would make a great stool!

►One of these may be tucked into a tool box somewhere. This vintage 6 foot folding ruler, with brass hinges was standard equipment for serious carpenters.

◄Vintage weights and balance scale with milk glass trays.

Caution

If ever there was a place where work gloves, mask and eye protectors are appropriate, this is it! Dress appropriately before beginning to clean up the garage. Lots of plant poisons and paint fumes exist so be sure the big door is open.

Garage	Keep	Sell	Bequest
Electrical Tools			
Hand Tools			

Garage	Keep	Sell	Bequest
Sports			
Equipment			
Auto			
Collectibles			
Other			

The Garage

This will likely be the last and least interesting place to sort and organize because it tends to be a catch-all for things we 'will deal with later'. License plates, rusty tins, tires, fertilizers, plant pots, broken tools and misplaced jar lids, boxes of this and piles of that accumulate, waiting to be 'dealt with'. First of all, toss away the obvious junk. No one wants a jar of old screws and nails, and nuts and bolts, so toss those out. Flower pots, unless they are high quality material and design, can go. Perhaps a school with a greenhouse program might be interested, but only if they are clean and not broken. Do you really want to go through all that work?

Toxic materials such as hardened cans of paint and stain, cleaners and polishes should be disposed of

▲Universal pressure tire gauge. These were once given away by garages and tire companies as appreciation gifts to loyal customers. This one still has its original leather case.

safely. Contact your local fire department and they will advise how and where to handle these items safely. Fertilizers and weed killers have no value either. They lose their strength after a year or two, and are actually hazardous to your health. Dispose safely.

Unless old screens and windows are still used on the house, they have no value. They can go. Tires can be recycled so can glass, tin, plastic, wire hangers, and so on and so forth. Check with the local recycle depot.

What *should* you look for? Tools and tool boxes, sports equipment, automobile memorabilia, and high quality ceramic flower pots have value.

Tools

For most men, the garage is their sanctuary away from the noise and hustle bustle of the day. It is a place where they work on their cars, work with power tools, make things, repair things and take things apart.

▲ 1911 door trim / router plane

Most of the tools and equipment were expensive to begin with and are still fairly valuable. Before giving them away, get an appraisal. Old woodworking tools, especially those with wood and metal parts and those with the owners initials impressed into the wood are prized. Exotic woods, like mahogany,

◄1900 plane

rosewood and oak are definitely valued. The STANLEY name is one that is drawing a great deal of attention lately. There are few books on the topic but many collectors interested in quality tools.

Old woodworking tools have a feel of quality about them. One can imagine a craftsman spending countless hours turning spindles for a cradle, finishing a tabletop or carving intricate designs into the side of a bookshelf or a chair back.

They may be rusty, but old tools, such as the early 1900 plane, the 1911 door trim/router plane, or ◄ this set of wood carving tools, are in demand by serious collectors.

Brian's Story

Brian did an appraisal on home contents shortly before the owners were preparing for a garage sale. All items were set out on tables, ready for the sale. As Brian passed through the garage into the house, he enquired about several tins holding bits of nails, screws, nuts, bolts and other assorted bits of this and that. The owner gave him permission to 'do whatever you want with those'. Thinking that Brian would keep the contents, the owner was surprised when he tipped the contents into the garbage, and proceeded to examine the dozen or so tins. They were old and some were rusty but it turns out, they were unique tobacco tins from the early 20's. The fifteen Long Tom Tobacco Co. tins were appraised at a value of $200-$250 US each.

► You may not find this particular lunch box, but you might find a similar one filled with nails and screws and other bits of nothing. Toss out the contents, and keep the lunch box. Dust it off and add it to the appraisal pile. These boxes are fetching upwards of $35 each. (this is one of the most mass produced lunch boxes - over 6,000,000 were made).

► Vintage 1954 Diamond professional pitching horseshoes set with original instruction sheet and box which adds considerably to the value of the set.

Vintage fishing theme postcards, ties, lures with original box, and a fishing basket (creel).

Creels, especially older ones, are considered prized pieces of folk art.

Collectors are keen to purchase any of these items to add to their collections. Decorators are interested in purchasing these items, to create atmosphere for lodges, bed and breakfasts, restaurants and private homes.

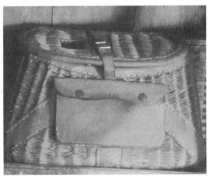

Sports Equipment

Fishing memorabilia is highly prized so before you price the old fishing tackle box full of old lures and reels at $10, look carefully. Names like CHUBB CREEK sound mysterious but lures by this company can fetch in excess of $200, especially if they are still in their original boxes. Art with a fishing theme, especially from the 18th and 19th century is fairly valuable as well.

Fish decoys can be traced to prehistoric times when cavemen enticed fish to the fishing holes cut into the ice. Crude examples of fish decoys can be seen in museums around the country. A more recent hand carved decoy from the 1930's, carved by Oscar Petersen of New York State, originally sold for fifty cents and was purchased at auction in the late 1990's for $12,000.

Watch for rods and reels made by Hardy of England. Split cane fly rods can fetch values in the thousands! old books on the subject.

The art of tying flies is highly respected amongst serious anglers, so flies, books, and anything dealing with this is of interest to collectors.

Old books about fishing are also prized. Pretty much any vintage item about or dealing with fishing is worth a second look.

▶This brook trout got away, but not before it was re-created in wood by an expert woodcarver who painstakingly painted it in realistic detail to be displayed for many to admire.

The Attic

In homes where the attic is bigger than a crawl space, it often becomes yet another place to store white elephants. It is easy to imagine children playing dress-up with clothing kept from another era, amongst an assortment of discarded and broken furniture and lamps, and trunks filled with someone else's memories. It is a nostalgic place and perhaps the kind of attic you are facing.

Victorian Wicker Chair from the late 1800's. Needs some restoration.
Value: $400 - 500

White elephant
The white elephant is believed to be sacred in some parts of the orient because it is such a rare animal. It is highly valued and at one time was considered property of the King (Thailand, formerly known as Siam). It was protected and cherished. A white elephant sale, however, is just the opposite: one is hard pressed to find a cherished item amongst the white elephants found there.

Attic	Keep	Sell	Bequest
Appliances			
Gadgets			
Dishes			
Clothing			

Attic	Keep	Sell	Bequest
Glassware			
Collectibles			
Paintings			
Pictures			
Wall			
decorations			
Furniture			
Family			
History			
Memorabilia			
Medals			
Albums			

▶A set like this can be very valuable, however, *Disney* is not as valuable as it used to be, but *Noma* is. Cords must be in remarkable condition (most dry out) and the box must be in good condition (not taped on every corner). The light covers should not have peeling decals. Prices, taking all the above into consideration, could be as high as $300 to the right collector.

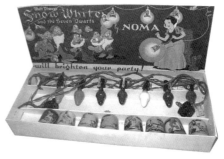

▶This unique lamp, with original red glass bulbs and brass base was found without its original shade. Extra bulbs, however, were found, each fetching a price of $35 or more.

◀ Crystal lamp with brass fittings and marble base.

◀Dionne Quintuplets calendar from 1938, is still collectible to some. Generally, old calendars are of interest to people wanting to commemorate a special event linked to that year. Paper products are hard to keep in pristine condition due to humidity and mold, however, in pristine condition, a find like this is a treasure.

The
Basement

Cobwebs! Laundry supplies and preserving equipment... jars and cans, pots and rusty old pans, plumbing bits and unidentified tools and hardware ... my oh my! Why anyone would think someone would want a cracked toilet seat is a mystery, however, chances are you will find one of these in the basement!

In the absence of an attic, the basement is the dumping place for boxes of old books, papers, and trunks of things from other generations. This can be a very scary place. It is also the first place that gets hit when there's a flood or a sewer backup, so knowing what's there and what it's worth is important.

Probably, there are stacks of empty boxes and bags. Dump them. Unless the boxes are valuable, like wooden orange crates or butter boxes, ordinary corrugated cardboard should be discarded. They are full of spores and other nasties waiting to attack your breathing. Get new lidded boxes for storing, and packing up possessions.

Basement	Keep	Sell	Bequest
Appliances			
Gadgets			
Tools			

Basement	Keep	Sell	Bequest
Collectibles			
Luggage			
Electrical			
appliances			
Furniture			
Sports			
equipment			

Appliances

Strangely enough, many people keep defunct, out-of-date appliances such as toasters, coffee pots and irons. Perhaps the intention was to have them repaired or use the parts for something else. More likely, they have

simply been forgotten and are just taking up space. Some old mixers and toasters are sought after but, they must be in pristine condition. Also look for original crock pots, soda mixers, and interesting tea kettles. Old coffee wheels and grinders are at a premium.

◀Many people tend to keep the bits and pieces after completing a home renovation. Many heritage homes are now being restored to original glory, and items, like these light switches from the 30's and 40's are in demand. So are glass doorknobs, brass light fixtures and tin ceiling tiles.

Luggage

Brian discovered a set of three pieces of rawhide luggage, originally purchased at Birks and still with the original Carson labels. They were owned by a past manager of a large store and were now destined for a garage sale for $50. Brian appraised the set for $500-$650.

Steamer trunks, on the other hand, are found in nearly every home and are not as dear in value unless in pristine condition.

◀Washboards such as this one, are quite common. Some have glass surfaces and some have metal. Value: $35

▶Graniteware canning kettle and Imperial canning jar. Old jars don't have much value, unless they have a beaver symbol on them, or are turning blue or purple in colour.

◀Tartan Tin Picnic basket, typical of the 1950's, usually filled with plastic plates, cups, cutlery and assorted containers for food items. Value: $40

▶Copper Kettle used for canning or heating water on a coal stove. Value is more for decorative interest than monetary.

Most of the items found on this page have more nostalgic value than monetary value, however, they are typical of the things one might find stuck in a corner somewhere in the basement, behind the boxes of papers and stacks of jars.

Additional Items	Keep	Sell	Bequest

The Appraiser Visit

Finally, the appraiser is at the door! Now the big work begins. When he starts to go through your home, you will hear terms such as the following:

Fair Market Value

This is the price that was paid the last time a particular item was available on the open market. For example, a cup and saucer may had a retail value of $60 when new. The pattern no longer is being made, but the fair market value remains $60.

Insurance Value

The value you should have pieces insured should they be damaged, lost or stolen. It is a common belief that the more expensive an item, the more money one needs to pay to insure an item. Increasing the contents value of the house is often enough to include specific items. It is a good idea to have lists, photos and any appraisal documents stored in a safe place such as a safety deposit box, should you need to deal with insurance issues.

Replacement Value

What will it cost for you to go out and buy an identical or similar item to replace the one you lost?

Collectible

This is an item up to 50 years old. If new, it is often produced in a limited quantity which should be clearly stated (number / how many produced). Pieces are referred to as *retired* once they are no longer produced. The original mold will be destroyed, making

Soapstone carvings all too often are found serving as doorstops rather than art. These pieces, valued at $1000 and upwards are unique. The bottom markings give important information about the artist, the art work and more!

By 1935, a large number of Canadian homes had a radio perhaps similar to this 1930 Litl Boy Crossley model. Isolated areas were linked to the outside world, and more importantly, news of the war was accessible. After the war, talk shows continued, along with favorites such as: *The Happy Gang, Hockey Night in Canada* and *Command Performance*. Antique radio clubs are alive and well, and radios such as this may be repaired, restored and enjoyed for many more years to come. However, parts are getting harder to find. Best to search out parts quickly if you intend to repair an antique radio.

older pieces more valuable, especially if they were made in small numbers. Other collectibles are items that were once common, affordable, and not meant to be valuable but have somehow survived intact. Often they have nostalgic value that strengthens the demand and produces an increase in cost. Just look at toys in original boxes, and dishes from the wear in the 30's. *Collectible* is what people want because it is fashionable again.

Heirloom

50 - 100 years old, or more than one generation old (for example; belonged to great grandmother). Heirlooms are treasures that have a great deal of sentimental value and often the replacement value is difficult to assess.

Antique

is anything that is more than 100 years old. The appeal for antiques depends on what is fashionable. Antiques were very much in demand the last twenty or so years, but interest is waning as younger generations want something more *retro*. In other words, they want the stuff from the 60's and 70's.

Fake

An item that has been made in the image of an older piece is a fake. It lacks the genuine characteristics of the original. For example, a vase may have the backstamp 'outside the glaze', whereas the original would be under the glaze. A piece of furniture, while it may appear Victorian, will have lighter weight woods used on drawer facings and may not be dovetailed.

Forgery

is an item that has been altered in some way to make it appear to be something else. For example, a bureau is converted to a desk, a vase to a lamp, or the bottom unit of a china cabinet does not match the top. In a case like this, the term 'married' is used which means two pieces are combined which have nothing to do with each other. In the case of paintings, some are being *printed* on canvas to mimic genuine art.

Reproduction

Given the desire of many collectors to have popular items such as *Fiesta* ware dishes, and *Tiffany* lamps, numerous factories have begun to reproduce pieces *in the style of Fiesta, Tiffany* and others. The copy should be clearly labeled as a reproduction, and often will be described as *in-the-style-of.* Reproductions should be priced reasonably. As a glut develops on the market, due to the great demand for a particular style, the cost of the genuine article drops. People are happy to buy a new reproduction at a fraction of the cost, rather than an original at an astronomical cost.

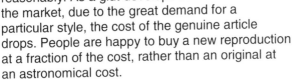

Turning cups over to determine age, maker and value, Brian assesses the value of seemingly ordinary cups and glassware, brought in by curious collectors. The good news is: there are treasures to be found in the kitchen cabinets!

Vintage

This term is often applied to anything of nostalgic (but not necessarily antique) value. For example, items from the fifties and sixties are vintage, as are items from the thirties and forties. Old pieces of jewelry, old dishes, lamps and old furniture are also vintage because they are well aged, preserved and still a delight to own.

Preparing for The Sale

You are now nearly ready to start your sale. Anyone may have up to two sales per year, according to the tax department without declaring income. First, there are some necessary steps to follow.

Defining the Sale

Apartment or Condo sale

If the estate sale is to be held in an apartment, condo or town house development, check first that the sale can actually be held. Some seniors complexes do not permit sales such as garage sales or estate sales, due to insurance concerns, high traffic and the general clutter created following a sale.

Sale by invitation only

You can drop notices into the suites or units in your building complex. Invite people to attend the sale at appointed times, which does not require street advertising and will alleviate traffic and parking concerns.

Sale in Your Home

Decide which area you will allocate for the sale: basement, family room, garage, or, if you are sizing down or selling the house, then the entire house will be used.

Details, Details, Details

Organizing the House as the sale venue

1. If the house is also being sold, have carpets cleaned. This will definitely improve the look and sales appeal of the house.
2. Wash the windows. If there is a smoker in the house, you might try various deodorizer sponges which absorb odors. Do not use air fresheners or plug in

deodorants. In addition to not removing the smoky odours, they also cause serious problems for people with allergies to fragrances. Plug-ins have also been known to catch fire. If the interior is really bad, repainting might be the only option.

3. Get mats or runners to serve as paths to direct traffic throughout the house, and to protect the carpets. These can be rented at a nominal fee or purchased quite reasonably at hardware and home centers.

Security

If the house is going to be completely unoccupied, be sure that a security system, if installed, is still functioning, that lights can still be left on a timer, drapes left slightly open, and other signs of occupancy are evident. BEWARE of DOG signs posted in front and back windows, on the garage door and gate also serve as a deterrent to potential thieves and vandals.

Pricing items for an estate sale. Notice the size of the tags and the placement of tags inside goblets and vases.

Permits

Some communities require a permit be purchased before a sale of any kind can be advertised and held. Check with the local community association or town office or by-law office, to get these details. Failure to do so could result in hefty fines.

Toss 'n Sort Day

It's a good idea to get help. If you have hired a professional, a toss' n sort day will be included.

View of book and recording section at an estate sale. Everything is tagged and sorted for easy viewing by customers and quick inventory check by staff. Notice the size of the tags on the big items. Make them big enough to be visible at a glance.

Table arrangement up for an estate sale.

Otherwise, you will have to sort items to prepare for pricing. You will need boxes for charity, giving to family and for tossing out. At the same time, you sort items for sale into boxes with the prices listed on the front. For example:

$2.50	$7.50	$11.50	$17.50

gradually building up to the more expensive small items. When pricing, build in at least a 20% discount. In other words, expect to sell a $7.50 item for $5.00. For more expensive items, determine what's fair. Do some phoning and research for similar items, then add 20%. Do not over price!

Equipment

Rent or borrow at least four- six large tables for items that will be displayed for sale. Cover them with white tablecloths. These can be rented and are definitely superior to an arrangement of saw horses, boards and old sheets, which suggests a garage sale rather than estate sale. This is where the professional excels. They can set the sale up for you, and make everything look great. How things are displayed may mean the difference between a sale and non-sale.

Pricing

Once everything is sorted, all items need to be tagged using at least 1"x 2 1/2" tags and a black felt pen. Have one person price, while another attaches tags to items. Use bigger tags for bigger items. (see photos page 132) Place tags inside cups and bowls, and tape or tie to bigger items.

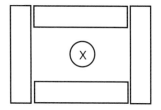

The square arrangement enables one person to deal with four tables at a time. The three table arrangement uses wall space for pictures and wall decorations. Both arrangements encourage good viewing by the customers.

Arranging and Displaying

For items to sell, they must be arranged in such a way that they look attractive. Dust doesn't sell, so dust, and if necessary, wash items before displaying them. Arrange the tables in a square, draped with pressed white cloths. Tables should be in the center of the room, or three tables set again the wall. (diagrams above). One person can be stationed at this group of tables. This is a good place to put better quality items, such as jewelry (in a protective display case which can be rented or borrowed) or expensive crystal, china and figurines.

Larger pieces should be arranged around the perimeter (XXX, see above) with electrical items on an additional table by a plug-in so that they can be tested.

Arrange items thematically, such as all Christmas items together, sound and video, books, china and so forth. Put all bedding and blankets in a bedroom, on a stripped down bed so people can see the mattress they are buying. Be sure bedding is clearly labeled by size (double, queen) and use safety pins to attach tags. Towels should be bundled and tied in sets by colour.

Again, use safety pins to attach the price tags which also lists each piece and size in the bundle.

It is imperative every single item be price tagged.
On sale day you should be collecting money, not guessing the price of an item. Having set prices also removes the tiresome 'make me an offer' conversation. Assuming all items are priced and arranged in an appealing manner, you are now ready to consider advertising and sale dates.

After the first day, items should be consolidated, and rooms closed off which are no longer needed. Be prepared to reorganize at the end of the first day.

Sale Dates

Who is available to help you? When are the most people able to come? Don't even think about having a sale during a major event like a long weekend. Most people likely have other plans and won't come.

Best sale days are Thursday, Friday, and half-price day on Saturday. About 85% of people start their sales on Friday, so you have stiff competition, therefore Thursday is a better start-date. Start the sale at 10 AM and finish at 6 PM to enable people returning from work to drop in. Adhere to these times and don't open or close early. If the weather is an issue, be prepared to call the whole thing off. Have a back up plan to deal with this, especially if the sale is in October or November. Make plans to try again a week or two later. Check with the weather office. They will tell you if there is a 50% chance of rain or snow based on patterns of the last thirty years. If that appears to be the forecast, select new dates. Once the date is established and staff confirmed, you are ready to start promoting the sale.

Sales Team

You need reliable people to help you, and you need to have a back-up plan and some major policies in place. Once you have selected your staff, make a chart with phone numbers, and confirm, confirm, confirm!! Have a few extra people for back up in case weather or health issues preventing someone from coming. It happens!

Staff required

    * someone posted in every room where items are displayed. It may not be necessary to have so many people. If the sale is in multiple rooms, put the large items that can't be shop-lifted, in the back rooms. Put all the smaller items on three or four tables butted together in the front room. (see page 134) If you have items in the garage, place a person there too.

    * a cashier and an assistant. Have a wrapping table close by to enable customers to wrap and pack their own purchases.

    * a manager who will float throughout the day (the

This impressive display represents only a fraction of more than 50 years of treasures gathered by an enthusiastic doll collector. Whose responsibility is it to find out what all this is worth?

one and only person authorized to negotiate prices and make deals).

*a traffic director posted at the door to greet and direct people through the house, especially in the first one - two hours of the sale. The entrance and exit should be the same. The first day is the busiest, so have two people on this post to spell each other off.

You also need people to stay afterwards to pack, clean and clear on the last day. An average sale requires six - eight people for the first day and four - six for the final day.

Before the sale begins, establish shifts, assign areas, and invite the team to come early enough on the sale day to review policies, preview the items, and generally get organized.

Advertising

Newspapers

An ad in the paper generally attracts people who are looking for a great bargain and want items to resell for profit. The people you want to attend the sale are neighbours, friends and relatives, and people passing through who are attracted by your wonderful signs.

Fliers

This is the best way to bring people to your sale. Distribute fliers to all the households in the area (generally 3000 - 5000 are enough). Fliers may be hand-written (block letters) typed or produced with a desk-top publishing program. Ask the computer whiz-kids to help! Layout should include phrases such as:

* Not Advertised
* Never Had a Sale Before
* Collector for X years

* Everything tagged

* Must be Sold

* Moving or Sizing Down

If you are also selling the house, include a picture of the house on the top of the flier. Don't include the price but do detail some of the main features. Include a list of some of the items being sold, especially unique items that will attract collectors, or people seeking furniture deals, and list these on the bottom half of the flier.

Printing and Distributing Fliers

Go to at least three printers to get a quote. Usually, the greater the number printed, the cheaper the price which is generally between three and five cents a page. They can also fold for an additional penny. Ask the printer to bundle or separate the fliers in stacks of 100.

Check with the post office about delivery costs. Ask for a map of your area which lists the total number of people by postal code. Examine the list and decide how many fliers you want to mail. Costs are minimal: about ten cents / flier. Total cost? Fifteen cents to bring a buyer to your sale. Not a bad deal at all. Allow at least ten days prior to the sale to get the printing and distribution done. Confirm deadlines for mailing to ensure timely delivery.

Brian and Donna working together to help a family sort through an assortment of life-time possessions.

Hint: if you are working with a realtor, ask them if they have a special printing and delivery rate that they can pass on to you. Their cost is often much better.

Pairing with a Realtor

If you are combining the sale of the home with the contents, INSIST that the realtor send a flier to the area, showing the home on the top, and contents on the bottom. This alerts your neighbours who may have friends or family wanting to move into the area, that a house is available.

> *Brian says:*
> *Contrary to what most realtors tell you, it is not better to leave the house packed or looking lived in. Clutter is clutter. A little house over furnished looks small. Insist on it being cleared out first.*

An average OPEN HOUSE notice on the street may attract ten - twenty prospective clients while a HOME AND CONTENTS sale flier attracts hundreds.

Parking

There will be a lot of traffic, so contact the neighbours well ahead of time, to alert them that additional traffic will be happening on sale day and be sure to secure their support to use space in front of their home and / or their driveway. The last thing you need on sale day is to get into a huge battle with neighbours about traffic! If necessary, post appropriate signs or assign someone to serve as a traffic director.

Signage

One of the biggest mistakes people often make is to make a small sign that is crammed with too much information. The sign is posted on a street corner and people driving by are expected to read all the details in one quick pass. Use fluorescent poster board, which measures 22" x 28". Write in large block letters with a wide felt pen, called Magnum 44 Permanent Marker by Stanford. Make at least three signs: one for the front of the home, and at least two to be placed in strategic places such as major intersections leading to the home.

ESTATE
SALE

1234 - 5th
Ave.

Oct. 10 - 13

Poster paper will not stand up alone so attach it to a stable backing such as 1/4" plywood. Don't use cardboard or staple the poster to trees and light posts. Construct the sign boards as follows: Drill two holes at the top, and two at the bottom. Run one rope through the top, and another through the bottom, which is long enough to secure the sign to a post or tree. You will need six or more of these, depending on how difficult it is to find the house. Signs at the front of the house should list dates, times with a ESTATE SALE heading. Signs on the street should simply state ESTATE SALE, address and the date, with an arrow pointing in the appropriate direction. Make another

ESTATE SALE

SALE NOT
UNTIL
THURSDAY
OCTOBER
10TH
NO EARLY
SALES

sign for the front and one for the back door that both state:

These signs should be placed on the Sunday afternoon prior to the Thursday sale. Put at least two signs at intersections but not too far away from the edge of the road. They need to be read! Check periodically over the next few days to make sure they haven't fallen over or been stolen. Yes, it happens. People steal sign boards.

The day of or late the night before the sale, put

out the signs with the arrows. Assign someone to take care of the signs. It is a huge task and needs someone willing to make several trips to place, check and replace signs as needed.

Finally, everything is priced, fliers distributed, signs out .... you are ready!

Have staff come at least 45 minutes prior to opening, and ask them not to park close to the house. Customers will need easy access to their vehicles to cart all their purchases away! Use that early time to preview the sale, review assignments and general policies.

Countdown Checklist

1. Pre-order a sandwich tray, avoiding eggs, tuna, salmon. Pick up trays the night before the sale. Purchase soft drinks and water for the staff. No alcoholic beverages.
2. Get the cash box float organized.
3. Set up the cash area.
4. Buy brown wrapping paper and bags of various sizes. Do not use recycled bags. Keep paper under the table and bags beside the cashier.
5. Set up the adding machine / calculator, with receipt books and several pens, stapler, scotch tape and masking tape.
6. Print name tags for staff. They're not necessary, but it helps customers know who they can ask about details and who is in charge of a particular area. A first name with 'ASK ME' is enough to identify your staff to customers.
7. Provide a place to go for a quiet break. If necessary, put a sign on a door to a room 'PRIVATE', and make that the retreat room for your staff.
8. HAVE FUN! This sale is just one step towards

moving on. All the serious planning and details are finished. The day should be stress-free because of all your meticulous organization. Enjoy.

After the Sale
Final Clean-Up

There will be things that need to be packed to donate. Be sure that arrangements have been made prior to the sale, for either pick up or for delivery of these items. Have charity numbers at hand. Many will come and pick up items from you, if you have planned this ahead of time. Most will list the items for donation using the prices already on them and issue a tax receipt. Do NOT leave boxes of items by the trash bin for garbage day. This is an open invitation to vandals and thieves that the house is empty or unoccupied.

Signs

Take down all the signs. If left, they may become an invitation for vandals and thieves as well.

Getting Your Own Estate in Order

Unfortunately, too many people pass on before considering the state of their affairs and making arrangements for their possessions. Most people have a will in place, stating that they bequest 'all their worldly goods to … ', however, have you *looked* at your worldly goods lately?

This book should have given you some ideas about what you can do to make it easier for your children and heirs when the time comes for your estate to be dismantled. You have spent a life time accumulating and it is your responsibility to decide what needs to be done. Don't count on your children to even want a quarter of what you intend to give them. According to Stats Canada, we can expect to live at least to age 79, and definitely many live well into the eighties and nineties. That means our children will be in their sixties and seventies when they finally get that set of china or that doll collection. Chances are they really don't want it any more because they have their own. Don't assume, however. Ask them. They may surprise you.

If you do have items you wish to pass on, invite the intended person for lunch and present them with the item carefully wrapped in a special box and with a note included about the history of the piece and its value. You will have the satisfaction of knowing the receiver can enjoy their legacy now and hopefully, their response will be a gift for you. It's so much nicer to receive a gift from a living person!

Appraise and identify the rest of the items for where they go and to whom. Sell what you can, give people what you want them to receive now, and get rid of the rest. You can get some extra cash out of the situation, and use it for your enjoyment now!

Choosing an Executor

An executor has a tremendous amount of work to do, which can be stressful as they deal with all the details of your life. Make provision to have the executor paid for their work as they will be spending countless hours and likely be making many trips until all details are settled to the satisfaction of your final wishes. Executors can easily spend 100 or more hours dealing with these details. Why would you expect them to do it for free?

Organize all personal papers, along with a record of bank accounts, stocks, bonds, and investments, in a safe place for them to access easily. There is nothing more stressful and heartbreaking than having to search for such details only to discover that someone's estate is in less than good order.

A Final Word

No one wants to think about their own ending, but taking care of details should be on everyone's priority list. Many families are separated by great distances, leaving them less informed about the values and priorities of parents and siblings. Legal hassles can arise and tie up matters for years at a time. That should be enough to make you want to take care of details now. Take time now to deal with the hard questions, make the difficult decisions, and sort and organize as much as you can so that you are not leaving stress, challenges and potentially long years of frustration and disappointment as part of your legacy.

Brian is often called to do appraisals and finds that a garage sale is also being planned. It is here that he often sees treasures tagged at ridiculously low prices because the kids just don't have the time or the interest to sort through the mess and contract a professional appraiser. Lighten your burden and lighten the burden of your heirs. They will be grateful that you loved them enough to take care of these matters for them. Besides, if you don't wait until you die to have *your* estate sale, you can take the cash now and possibly enjoy a little better quality living that is your right to enjoy!

It is Brian's greatest desire and mission to ensure that you get what it's worth while you can still enjoy it.

◄This unusual piece consists of a stand and plant pot (jardinière) surrounded by flamingos in shades of yellows and browns. Suspected to be Majolica, this huge unsigned piece has a few chips which devalues it considerably. Purchased for $1 at a garage sale, this piece is valued at $3000 in its present condition.

▲Tomato Teapot and creamer. Once popular, these brightly coloured sets are again in demand.

◄This 1915 stuffed bear, in mint condition, was made by a company called: Terrys. This is a highly collectible, and valuable little bear!

Brian Lehman

Brian's interest in artifacts began in 1964, after he'd made some bad purchases at his first collectibles auction. Determined never to over pay again, he set out to educate himself about collectibles, heirlooms and antiques. Several hundred auctions and volumes of reference books later, he began teaching students eager to learn what he'd learned.

With furniture refinishing techniques added to his expertise, he opened his shop: "Toys from the Attic" in Calgary in 1987. In 1994 he closed the store, to avoid conflict of interest and took on more appraisal work. During Alberta's Heritage Day in 1988, **CBC** radio invited Brian to talk about collectibles, and he soon became a regular on **CBC** Calgary's **The Home Stretch** and **CBC's Wild Rose Forum** as well as **CTV television.**

Since then, Brian has appeared on **CBC** Television, **CHED** (Edmonton) and **CJCY** (Medicine Hat) **CBC Midday Express, QR77 The Rutherford Show, The Terry Moore Show, Global's Breakfast show,** and **ACCESS Help TV.**

"What's It Worth Brian?" heard weekly on AM radio **QR770** in Calgary, and Edmonton's **630 CHED**, premiered in 1997, and is broadcast throughout western Canada and the US. A call to Brian always yields a history lesson as well as an appraisal of value. If he can't give you information, he'll tell you who can.

Brian Lehman lives in Calgary, Alberta with his soul mate "the lovely Donna" and two great children. Brian will do in-home appraisals to help clients decide what to do with their 'stuff'. Contact the lovely Donna, at *Brian Lehman Evaluations*: 403-249-7333 to book an appointment. He travels extensively for appraisal work, and is also available for antique events to do what he loves best: telling people '*what it's worth.*'

Helen Raczuk

met Brian Lehman in 2000, at the urging of her brother Terry. He recognized Brian had something to say, and believed that Helen was the one to put those thoughts into print.

'I can write about children learning, I can teach children to read, but what do I know about collectibles and antiques?' she argued. Turns out she knew a bit and has learned even more during this collaborative process which has unleashed a tremendous respect and interest for things older than her! Passionate about stories, it is a natural extension to learn the story behind a dish and the person who owned it. It's history, it's family, it's tradition - things that Helen cherishes. Helen, Brian and Donna have become good friends as a result of this project. She intuitively knows how Brian thinks and would like his thoughts expressed. This is her first non-school related publication, but, she hopes, not the last.

After teaching school for more than twenty years, Helen established *U Otter Read It Educational Resources*, with a friend and colleague in 1996. Their goal was to create literacy resources that were both educationally sound and Canadian. Since then, more than twenty eight publications have been produced with plans for many more! To learn more about these books, visit www.uotter.com, phone 780-962-9854 or email Helen: helen@uotter.com.

Helen lives in Spruce Grove where she runs her publishing company. She continues to travel extensively throughout Western Canada, Eastern USA and Singapore, to work with teachers and share her excitement about children's books and literacy.

Bibliography

Ewing, Alexander Crum. The Fountain Pen, A Collectors Companion. London, Quintet Publishing Ltd., 1997.

Franklin, Linda Campbell. 300 Years of Kitchen Collectibles. Alabama, Books America Inc., 1984.

Kovel, Ralph and Terry. Kovels' New Dictionary of Marks. New York N.Y. Crown Publishers, 1986.

Marks, Mariann Katz. Majolica. Paducah Kentucky. Collector Books, 1996.

McCawley, Patricia. Glass Paperweights. London, Charles Letts Books Ltd., 1975.

Pearson, Sue. Miller's Dolls and Teddy Bears. London. Mitchell Beazley Int. Ltd., 1992.

Sheehan, Laurence. The Angler's Life. New York. Clarkson Potter Publishers, 2000

Swedberg, Robert W. & Harriett. Furniture of the Depression Era. Paducah N.Y. Collector Books. 1990.

Appraising a garage sale find, Brian was able to give this avid bargain hunter some happy news. Her purchase was worth more than 142 times what she had originally paid.

To book Brian Lehman for an in-home appraisal, or event:
Phone: 403-249-7333
Listen to Brian on
630CHED Radio in Edmonton
QR770 in Calgary
and watch for his many on-location events across the country.

Brian with June
Evans, from *That's
Crafty* near
Rosebud Alberta;
another one of his
favourite on-
location events.

To learn more about Helen Raczuk and her literacy materials
and workshops for teachers and parents,

visit www.uotter.com
Phone 780-962-9854
email: helen@uotter.com
and watch for a seminar at a PD day or
teachers conference in your city or district.

Order additional copies: please provide all details* to complete your order.

Qty. _____   Price $24.95   Subtotal [   ]

*Name _____

*Address _____

_____

_____

*Phone _____

Email _____

Shipping and Handling:**   Order total: _____
Add $7.00 for the first book,
$1.00 for each additional copy.   Shipping: _____

                                         GST: _____
**Please note: prices subject to change without notice.
                                         Total: _____

Method of Payment

☐ Check

☐ Visa

☐ MasterCard

*Name and Address on credit card MUST
be identical to Name and Address on order*   Thankyou!
form to ensure payment is approved.   *Brian & Helen*

Credit Card # _____   Exp. date _____

Signature _____

          Fax 780-962-9882   Phone 780-962-9854

          OR Mail: U-Otter Read It
                          11 Miller Place
                          Spruce Grove, Alberta
                          T7X 2N1